SCOTLAND'S M

Allan Morrison

'Whaur's Yer Wullie Shakespeare Noo?'

NEIL WILSON PUBLISHING LTD. GLASGOW, SCOTLAND

Published by Neil Wilson Publishing Ltd
303a The Pentagon Centre
36 Washington Street
GLASGOW
G3 8AZ
Tel: 0141-221-1117
Fax: 0141-221-5363
E-mail: nwp@cqm.co.uk
http://www.nwp.co.uk/

A catalogue record for this book is available
from the British Library.

10 8 6 4 2 1 3 5 7 9

ISBN 1-897784-49-X

With grateful thanks to Craig Morrison, Robert and
Grace Henderson, Jim McLelland, Marion Potter,
Joyce Walker and Archie Wilson.

Typeset in Bodoni
Designed by Mark Blackadder
Printed by Cromwell Press

CONTENTS

Introduction iv

11TH CENTURY	1000–1099	1
12TH CENTURY	1100–1199	13
13TH CENTURY	1200–1299	26
14TH CENTURY	1300–1399	39
15TH CENTURY	1400–1499	54
16TH CENTURY	1500–1599	68
17TH CENTURY	1600–1699	85
18TH CENTURY	1700–1799	102
19TH CENTURY	1800–1899	120
20TH CENTURY	1900–1999	139
THE NEW MILLENNIUM	2000	156

INTRODUCTION

As Scotland is about to leave behind one millennium and enter the next, I decided that this was a propitious time for some reflection on our past. The result is a compilation of events and historical milestones from the last 1000 years of Scottish history which range from the straightforward to the plain daft. *'Whaur's Yer Wullie Shakespeare Noo?'* is a timely last chance to pause and look back.

In a very few instances, where there are only fragments of detail, I have had to use a little judgement in determining the actual year of an event, but for the greater part, the dates and the events are correct and the people involved in them were real.

I hope that this wee book will encourage all readers to study Scottish history in greater depth and so have a better understanding of how this small country has contributed so much to the world. This book is not just for Scotland's present inhabitants, but also for the many people throughout the world who are proud of their Scottish heritage. This then, is the story of a small nation with a large and enduring fascination.

Allan Morrison,
Greenock.
January 1998

1000 The start of the new millennium and the fourth year of the reign of the King of Scots, Kenneth III, known as 'The Grim'. King Ethelred's English forces ravaged the Kingdom of Strathclyde and wrested Lothian from Kenneth's control.

1001 Duthal, who became Saint Duthus, was born on the south side of the Dornoch Firth.

1002 The King of Scots, Kenneth III, and his nobles, went on a pilgrimage to Rome.

1003 Kenneth III led his forces into Northumbria, to plunder.

1004 MacBeth, the future king and the son of Findlaech, the Mormaer of Moray (provincial ruler), was born.

1004 Birth of Macbeth

1005 Kenneth III, who had reigned since 997 was killed by Malcolm at Monzievaird, near Perth. Malcolm became Malcolm II, King of Scots.

1006 Malcolm II lost the Battle of Forres, against Sweno, son of King Harold of Denmark.

1007 The marriage of Bethoc, the eldest daughter of Malcolm II, to Crinan, Abbot of Dunkeld. (Their son later became King Duncan I).

1008 The marriage of the younger daughter of Malcolm II, to the Earl Sigurd of Orkney.

1009 The birth of Thorfinn, the eldest son of Sigurd, Earl of Orkney.

1010 Battle of Carron, near Dufftown, when Malcolm II won a major victory over a Viking invasion force.

1011 The monastery of Mortlach, in Banffshire, was established by Malcolm II.

1012 Forces, under Malcolm II, attacked several Northumbrian townships.

1013 Malcolm II assumed rule of the region of Mar in Aberdeenshire.

1014 The death of Sigurd, the Earl of Orkney. He was fighting on the side of Sitric, the Norse King of Dublin, against the Irish high King, Brian Boru, at the Battle of Clontarf.

1015 Malcolm II's grandson, Thorfinn, became Scotland's vassal. His lands of Sutherland and Caithness came under Malcolm.

1016 Unsuccessful attack on Durham, by Malcolm II's troops.

1017 Thorfinn, the Earl of Orkney, age eight, joined the court of his grandfather, Malcolm II, King of Scots.

1018 Malcolm II won the Battle of Carham against English forces, under Earl Uhtred of Bamburgh. As a result Malcolm annexed Lothian from England and claimed the Tweed as a Scottish river.

1019 By order of Malcolm II, Edinburgh Castle, (Dun Eiden) was no longer deemed to be a frontier stronghold.

1020 The son-in-law of Malcolm II, Findlaech, Mormaer of Moray, was slain by his nephews.

1021 By order of Malcolm II, the Scottish border was extended beyond the Solway.

1022 Northumberland was given to England, and Lothian was then ceded to Malcolm II.

1023 Establishment by Malcolm II of the thanes of Cawdor, Angus and Fortingall. (Centres presided over by a 'royal' official for the extraction of various dues.)

1024 Further development of thanes in Glentilt, Clave, O'Neil and Aboyne.

1025 The church of St John was built, near Crovie, Banffshire, as appreciation for the defeat of Viking raiders nearby.

1026 Malcolm II established thanes at Arbuthnot, Cowie and Birse.

1027 Thorfinn, the Earl of Orkney, made a claim to a third of the total Kingdom of Scotland.

1028 MacBeth, King of Scots, married Gruoch, the widow of Gillacomgain of Moray.

1029 The marriage of Duncan and the cousin of Siward, the Earl of Northumbria.

1030 Invasion of Scotland by the armies of King Canute. Malcolm II was forced to submit for a limited period.

1031 Birth of Donald , who became Donald III, 'The Fair', son of Duncan I and younger brother of Malcolm III, 'Canmore'. Donald claimed the throne in 1093.

1032 The infant Malcolm 'Canmore' was taken on a visit to the English court of Edward the Confessor.

1033 Kenneth III was slain by Malcolm II.

1034 Death, at Glamis, of Malcolm II, thereby bringing the House of Alpin to an end. His grandson, Duncan I, became King of Scotland, though not of Orkney, Shetland or the Western Isles which remained in Scandinavian hands.

1035 Duncan I sent messages of goodwill to the new King of Norway, Magnus the Good.

1036 Defeat of Duncan I's forces by Thorfinn, Earl of Orkney, at a battle in Aberdeenshire.

1037 A second battle was fought in Aberdeenshire where Duncan I 's troops were again defeated by Thorfinn.

1038 Battle in Sutherland where Duncan's spearmen were beaten off by Thorfinn's forces.

1039 A siege on Durham, by Duncan I's army, proved fruitless.

1040 MacBeth killed his cousin, Duncan I, at the Battle of Pitgavey, near Elgin; MacBeth became king.

1041 MacBeth and his queen, Gruoch, granted endowments to the Culdees of the Island of Lochleven for prayer and intercession.

1042 MacBeth defeated Viking raiders at the Battle of Kinghorn.

1043 Duncan I's son, Malcolm Canmore, ('Big Head'), who became king in 1057, was sent to Northumbria to live with his uncle, Earl Siward.

1044 A visit was made to Argyll by the Irish prince, Niall. The family later became the Clan MacNeil.

1045 The death of Crinan, Abbot of Dunkeld, who married Bethoc, daughter of Malcolm II and who was father of Duncan I. He was killed campaigning against MacBeth.

1046 The birth, in Hungary, of Margaret, daughter of Edward 'The Exile', the son of Edmund Ironside. Margaret married Malcolm III in 1069 and was ultimately canonised as Saint Margaret.

1047 Earl Thorfinn of Orkney sent ambassadors to greet the new King of Norway, Harald Sigurdson.

1048 Donations of ground were made throughout Scotland to church authorities, by MacBeth and his Queen Gruoch.

1049 The visitation of Earl Thorfinn of Orkney to King Svein in Denmark.

1050 MacBeth and Thorfinn, Earl of Norway, visited Rome on pilgrimage. MacBeth is said to have 'scattered alms like seedcorn' whilst in Rome.

1051 Earl Thorfinn made his seat of government the Borough of Birksay on the west mainland of Orkney.

1052 The death of Aaron Scotus, the music theorist. He was a Scottish benedictine who became Abbot of St Pantaleon and St Martins, Cologne. He was responsible for *'de regulis tonorum et symphoniarum'*.

Macbeth and Thorfinn
in Rome

1053 MacBeth and Thorfinn, Earl of Orkney, agreed a pact whereby Thorfinn held the 'Nine Earldoms' in Scotland, as well as the Hebrides and a large realm in Ireland.

1054 Battle of Dunsinane, when forces under Malcolm Canmore defeated an army led by MacBeth.

1055 Castle Sween, on the south side of Loch Sween, Argyll, was founded by the O'Neils.

1056 MacBeth gave lands on the lower Tweed to the Gordon family, (from Gourdon in Querly, France), for their support in Scottish campaigns.

1057 MacBeth was killed by Malcolm Canmore at the Battle of Lumphanan in Aberdeenshire. MacBeth's stepson, Lulach, became king for four months.

1058 Malcolm Canmore killed Lulach at Strathbogie. Son of Duncan I, Canmore was crowned King Malcolm III.

1058 Coronation of
Malcolm Canmore
('Bighead')

1059 The Bishop of St Andrews granted the church of Markingh, and all its land, to St Serf and the Culdees of the Island of Lochleven.

1060 The birth of Duncan I, the eldest of the three sons of Malcolm III's marriage to Ingibiorg.

1061 Malcolm III invaded and plundered Northumbria.

1062 Pilgrimage to Rome by Malcolm III and his court.

1063 Incursion, by troops under Malcolm III, into the northern counties of England.

1064 Summer campaign by army of Malcolm III in Northumbria.

1065 The death of Earl Thorfinn of Orkney, age 75.

1066 The two sons of Thorfinn, the Earl of Orkney, fought on the side of Harald Hardrada, King of Norway, at the Battle of Stamford Bridge.

1067 Malcolm III of Scotland donated Dunbar to Cospatric, the Earl of Northumberland.

1068 The death of Malcolm's queen, Ingibiorg.

1069 Malcolm III married the Saxon, Margaret (see 1046). They had a family of six sons and two daughters.

1070 The north-western lands of England plundered by Malcolm III and his troops.

1071 Margaret escaped across the River Forth from troops of William the Conqueror. At Margaret's instigation, free passage was given thereafter to pilgrims en route to St Andrews, via the 'Queen's Ferry'.

1072 Following a major invasion by the English king, William the Conqueror, Malcolm III and William met at Abernethy where a pact was agreed. Malcolm's son, Duncan, age three, was handed over as a hostage.

1073 Malcolm III and Queen Margaret granted the town of Ballecristin to the monks of Lochleven.

1074 Birth of Edgar, the fourth son of Malcolm III and Margaret. Edgar became king in 1097.

1075 The birth of Malcolm and Margaret's son, Eithelred; he was to become the Abbot of Dunkeld.

1076 Invasion of the English northern counties by Malcolm III, thereby breaking the Treaty of 1072.

1077 The birth, in Dunfermline, of Alexander, the fifth son of Malcolm III and Queen Margaret. He would become king in 1107.

1078 Queen Margaret moved her household from St Andrews to Edinburgh Castle.

1079 Malcolm III again breaks the Treaty of Abernethy and invades Northumbria, penetrating as far as the River Tyne.

1080 The foundation, by Queen Margaret, of a Benedictine priory in Dunfermline . It became Dunfermline Abbey in 1128.

1081 St Oran's Chapel, the earliest existing ecclesiastical building on Iona, was built on the instructions of Queen Margaret.

1082 The construction of a new castle on the Tyne was started by Robert, son of William I of England. It was designed to hold forces for use against the Scots.

1083 Work commenced on Carlisle Castle. It was built to complement the new castle on the Tyne and hold a garrison for the defence of northern England against the Scots.

1084 The birth of David I. He was the sixth son of Malcolm III and Queen Margaret.

1085 The death of Malsnectai, son of Lulach, who had been killed by Malcolm III in 1058. Malsnectai had been Lord of Moray until ousted by Malcolm in 1078 and ended his days as a monk.

1086 St Vegean's parish church was built in Arbroath. It contains the 'Drosten Stone', a cross-slab with Pictish Christian synbols.

1087 The hostage Duncan (see 1072), son of Malcolm III's first marriage, was freed.

1088 A successful campaign in Northumbria by Malcolm III and his forces.

1089 The church of Dunning, in Perthshire, was founded by Queen Margaret.

1090 The marriage of Lady Octreda of Dunbar to Duncan, who became Duncan II in 1094.

1091 As a result of Malcolm III again invading Northumbria, the King of England, William II, (Rufus) marched north into Lothian, where peace terms were agreed.

1092 William II of England sent troops over the border from the garrison at Carlisle. As a result all Cumbria south of the Solway was wrested from Scotland.

1093 Malcolm III of Scotland and his army invaded England, once too often, and were trapped near the River Alne. Malcolm and his son Edward were killed. Malcolm's queen, Margaret, on hearing the news was overcome and died. Malcolm was succeeded by his brother Donald Bane, 'The Fair', who immediately banished all English from the Scottish court.

1094 Duncan, the son of Malcolm III, marched north with an army to claim the throne. He ousted Donald III and for a few months reigned as king. He was killed at Mondynes, in a feud with his half-brother, Edmund. Donald III was restored to the throne. (Duncan is buried on Iona.)

1095 Angus, son of Aethelred, became the ruler of Moray on the death of his uncle, Maelsnechtai.

1096 Edgar, Malcolm's fourth son, was put in charge of an English regiment by William II of England.

1097 Edgar, the oldest surviving son of Malcolm and Margaret, marched north with his army. Donald III was overthrown, blinded and imprisoned. Edgar became king.

1098 Expedition by Magnus Barelegs, the Viking King of Norway, to strengthen his hold over Shetland, Orkney and the Western Isles. He had a vessel dragged across the isthmus of Kintyre at Knapdale, to symbolise his possession of the Isles.

1098   Expedition by Magnus Barefoot

1099 Edgar ceded the Western Isles to Magnus Barelegs. (Magnus Barelegs is considered by some to have worn an early version of the kilt.)

12TH CENTURY

1100   The marriage took place of Matilda, the daughter of Malcolm III and Margaret, to Henry I of England, the younger son of William the Conqueror.

1101   The Bruce family, from Normandy, were given various royal manors and lands by Henry I of England.

1102   The death, in prison, of Donald III, (Donald Bane the Fair). He was buried in Iona.

1103   Birth of Robert de Montgomerie who, after marrying a daughter of Walter 'The Steward', was given a grant to the lands of Eaglesham in Renfrewshire.

1104   Edgar was presented with an elephant by returning crusaders.

1104   King Edgar presented with an elephant

1105 A church was founded in Ednam by 'Thor the Long'; it was in honour of St Cuthbert.

1106 The marriage of Mary, daughter of Malcolm I and Margaret, to Eustace, the Count of Boulogne.

1107 Death of Edgar, (who was unmarried). His brother, Alexander, was crowned king.

1108 Forces under Alexander I quashed a rebellion by the people of Moray.

1109 On the orders of Alexander I, the annals of Iona were stored in the tower of Restenneth Priory, near Forfar.

1110 Alexander I purchased six Arabian horses for the royal stables.

1111 The founding of the Abbey of Selkirk by David, who became David I in 1124. (David ruled southern Scotland with the title, 'Earl', during the reign of Alexander I.)

1112 Alexander I had St Margaret's chapel built on the highest point of the castle rock, in Edinburgh.

1113 Marriage of the future David I to Matilda, the widow of Simon de Senlis and grand-neice of William the Conqueror.

1114 A Charter was drawn up by Alexander I, to recognise the founding of the Abbey of Scone by Augustinian Canons.

1115 The death of Turgot, Prior of Durham, who had been appointed Bishop of St Andrews by Alexander I in 1109.

1116 The parish of Livingston in West Lothian was founded by Leving, a merchant from Flanders.

1117 St Magnus was slain on the Isle of Egilsay. He was the joint Earl of Orkney with his cousin Haakon (who murdered him). St Magnus is buried in Kirkwall Cathedral.

1118 David I's French tutor, John, was appointed Bishop of Glasgow.

1119 A dictate was sent by the Archbishop of York, to all the Bishops in Scotland, stating that all future Bishops could only be appointed by him.

1120 The High Kirk of Edinburgh, later to become St Giles, was founded by Alexander I.

1121 The burghs of Berwick, Perth and Roxburgh were established.

1122 The death of Sybilla, the illegitimate daughter of Henry I of England, who had married Alexander I.

She is buried on 'The Island of Women' in Loch Tay, Perthshire.

1123 The hermit of Inchcolm Island, on the Firth of Forth, fed and sheltered Alexander I, when he was marooned on the island because of bad weather. As a result Alexander established an Augustinian Abbey on Inchcolm.

1124 The death of Alexander I at Stirling Castle and the accession to the throne of David I, age 44.

1125 Anglo-Norman feudalism was introduced into Scotland by David I.

1126 David I appointed a number of Anglo-French nobles into positions within the Scottish church.

1127 David I granted all the lands of Annandale to Robert de Brus.

1128 Dunfermline's Benedictine Priory was given the status of abbey by David I. It became the chosen burial place of eight kings (including Robert the Bruce), four queens, five princes and two princesses.

1129 A Royal Charter was given by David I, for a Burgh in Rutherglen.

1130 The Battle of Stracathro, when David I defeated Angus, the Earl of Moray, the grandson of Lulach.

1131 Notations in Gaelic were written in the margins and spaces within the Book of Deer. The book originated at the 6th-century Celtic monastery at

Deer, Aberdeenshire, and contains information on kings, landowners and events of that time. The Book of Deer was 'rediscovered' in Cambridge University library in 1715.

1132 Approval given by David I for the consecration, by Cormac, the Bishop of Dunkeld, of a church in honour of Christ and the apostle Peter.

1133 The Dominican Friary of Berwick was founded.

1134 Uprising in Moray and Angus led by Malcolm MacBeth, the illegitimate son of Alexander I. He was captured and imprisoned.

1135 David I ordered that the first coins be struck in Scotland since Roman times; they were silver pennies (sterlings).

1136 Forces under David I invaded England and seized control of Carlisle and Newcastle. Under the Treaty of Durham, David's son, Henry, was charged to hold Carlisle.

1137 Rognvald, the Earl of Orkney and nephew of Magnus, founded Kirkwall Cathedral. It was dedicated to St Magnus.

1138 Battle of the Standard at Cowton Moor, Northallerton, Yorkshire. David's army was defeated by an army under Thurstan, Archbishop of York

1139 Second Treaty of Durham, whereby David's son, Henry, was granted the whole of Northumbria with the exception of Newcastle and Bamburgh.

1140 Somerled, from the line of Kings of Dalriada, became ruler in Argyll and the Isles.

1141 David I, assisted the his niece, the Empress Matilda, stakes his claim to the English throne at the Battle of Winchester.

1142 The founding of Dundrennan Abbey in Kirkcudbrightshire by Fergus, Lord of Galloway. Its Cistercian monks came from Yorkshire.

1143 Birth of William I (The Lion), grandson of David I. William became king when he was 22.

1144 David I declared that in future the hereditary principle of succession would apply. This brought to an end to the Celtic system of tanistry, whereby the heir, or tànaiste to the throne, was elected by his peers.

1145 A charter was drawn up granting Henry, son of David I, the title of designated king.

1146 The Royal Mile in Edinburgh established by David I as 'the King's Hie Streete'.

1147 David I chose the site for the Augustinian Abbey of Cambuskenneth, near Stirling Castle.

1148 The stepson of David I, Waltheof, Earl of Northumberland, was appointed Abbot of Melrose.

1149 Agreement was reached between David I and Anjou, the Empress Matilda's son, on the ownership of lands in the North of England.

1146 Royal Mile established

1150 Dryburgh Abbey, St Boswells, Roxburgh, was
rebuilt by Augustinian monks from Premonstre in
France who came to Scotland under the patronage
of Hugh de Morville, Hereditary Constable of
Scotland. (Sir Walter Scott is buried at Dryburgh.)

1151 Crusade by Bishop William and Rognvald, Earl of
Orkney to the Holy Land. More of a piratical
expedition, they rounded up Christians for sale in
the slave markets, to raise funds to build Orkney
Cathedral.

1152 Death of David I's son, Henry, thereby predeceasing
his father. (Henry was the father of Malcolm IV and
William I.)

1153 Death of David I. Malcolm, his 11-year-old
grandson became Malcolm IV, under the
guardianship of Earl Duncan.

1154 Henry of Anjou, became Henry II of England and
made contact with the court of the boy king,
Malcolm IV.

1155 The Priory of Jedburgh was elevated to Abbey status.

1156 Somerled, who reigned in Argyll, defeated Godfrey, the Irish-Norse King of the Isles and Man, in a sea battle off Islay. He gained control of all the islands south of Ardnamurchan.

1157 At the treaty of Chester, Malcolm IV resigned the three counties of the North of England to Henry II of England; in return he received the Earldom of Huntingdon.

1158 Somerled's brother-in-law, Godred, fled to Norway to plead for support in his fight against Somerled. Norway opted to recognise Somerled as King of the Isles.

1159 Rebellion took place in Galloway against Malcolm IV.

1160 The Priory of Augustinian Canons, in Scone, was given Abbey status.

1161 Bishop Arnold, with the encouragement of Malcolm IV, began the construction of St Andrews Cathedral.

1162 Parish Rights were granted to the monks of Newbattle Abbey. (This ultimately became Monklands in Lanarkshire.)

1163 Chief Shaw Mackintosh and his clan went north, with Malcolm IV, to suppress a rebellion by the men of Moray.

1164 Somerled, the powerful 'King' of the West of Scotland, led an army against Malcolm IV, but was defeated and killed at the Battle of Renfrew.

1165 Malcolm IV, who was unmarried, died in Jedburgh. He was succeeded by his brother, William I.

1166 Death of Earl Cospatric of Dunbar, the son of the Earl of Northumberland. His stone coffin lies in Dalmeny Kirk.

1167 A Cistercian Abbey was founded in Coupar Angus.

1168 The Norman family of Hay, later to hold the Earldom of Errol, settled in Scotland.

1169 A Priory, dedicated to St Mirin (Mirren) in Paisley, was populated by Clunian monks from Wenlock in Shropshire. The Priory became an Abbey in 1219.

St Mirren

1170 Culzean Castle, near Maybole, Ayrshire, was founded by the Kennedy family. The castle was made over to the National Trust for Scotland in 1945 but a flat within the castle was reserved from 1946 onwards for the use of President Dwight D. Eisenhower. This was to recognise his services in World War Two.

1171 A Royal Charter was awarded to Aberdeen by king William I.

1172 Glasgow Cross erected at the foot of the High Street, after William I granted the burgh the right to hold a market each Thursday.

1173 William I agreed an alliance with the sons of Henry II of England, against their father. In return William received the new grant of the Earldom of Northumbria, as far as the Tyne.

1174 William I was taken prisoner by an English force whilst plundering in the North of England. He was imprisoned for five months but released after signing a treaty at Falaise, with Henry II of England, acknowledging Henry's feudal superiority.

1175 As part of the 1174 Treaty, the castles of Edinburgh, Roxburgh and Berwick were occupied by English garrisons.

1176 The lands of Kinnaird in Perthshire were granted to Radulfus Rufus, whose descendant became Lord Kinnaird.

1177 Alan Fitzalan was appointed the Steward of Scotland.

1178   The Abbey at Arbroath was founded by William I.
It was dedicated to St Thomas A' Becket. (In 1951
the Stone of Scone was temporarily deposited at the
Abbey having been taken from Westminster Abbey.)

1179   A campaign in Ross and the North of Scotland
by forces under William I. As a result Dunskaith
Castle, near Nigg, was built to support a garrison to
deal with local uprisings and Viking attacks.

1180   A Royal Charter was issued by William I, at the
old Eren Castle, in Nairnshire, to the Burgesses of
Inverness.

1181   Unsuccessful claim to the throne of Scotland by
Donald MacWilliam, grandson of Duncan II. It was
made on the basis that he was descended from
Malcolm III's first marriage, whereas William I was
from Malcolm's second marriage.

1182   The founding of Brodie Castle, near Forres, Moray,
the seat of the Brodies. (Although the Brodies
featured strongly in Scottish history they were never
'enobled'.)

1183   The St Leonard's Hospital in Perth was founded.

1184   After an inspection by the Sheriff of Haddington,
William I confirmed the lands of the monks of
Newbattle Abbey.

1185   William I acquired the Earldom of Huntingdon.

1186   William I married Ermengarde de Beaumont. They
had one son (Alexander II) and three daughters.

1187 Donald MacWilliam, the claimant to the throne (see 1181), was killed at the Battle of Mam Garbh, near Inverness, by Lord Roland of Galloway.

1188 The national independence of Scotland was confirmed by Papal Bull.

1189 After the death of Henry II of England, his son, Richard I agreed that Scotland was independent at the Treaty of Canterbury (called the 'Quitclaim'). The line of the border was also defined.

1190 Birth of Walter Comyn, the Earl of Menteith. In 1235 he incurred the wrath of Henry III of England by interfering in Irish affairs. At one time was deemed the most powerful figure in Scotland.

1191 The founding of Duart Castle on the Isle of Mull. It commanded the Sound of Mull and guarded Loch Linnhe.

1192 The Scottish Bishops appealed successfully to Pope Clementine to negate the provisions of the Treaty of Falaise, under which England had control of the Scottish Church.

1193 Bishop Jocelyn of Glasgow secured the agreement of William I, to hold an annual 'Glasgow Fair', for the eight days starting on the 7th of July.

1194 The rights of Scottish Kings to 'hospitality' at the English Court, was defined in a Charter signed by Richard I of England.

1195 William's proposal to the Scottish Lords that a
king's daughter 'carry Kingship', was not accepted.
(At this time William had daughters, but no son.)

1196 A further campaign by forces led by William I in
the North of Scotland. Royal castles were founded
at Dunskaith and Redcastle to dominate the
Cromarty and Beauly Firths.

1197 A mill was established at Hailes (Colinton), using
the 'Water of Leith'.

1198 Military Service was introduced under the feudal
system; 40 days in any one year were required by
those holding the feu.

1199 Richard I of England died and William I of Scotland
agreed to support John, Richard's brother,
provided John agreed to consider Scotland's claim
to Northumbria.

13TH CENTURY

1200 Formal negotiations took place between John, King of England and William I of Scotland, over rights to Northumbria.

1201 The burgh of Rutherglen was ordered, by William I, to double its annual three merks payment to the Deans of Glasgow Cathedral.

1202 The Earl of Orkney ordered that John Bishop, of Caithness, be blinded and have his tongue torn out.

1203 The Castle of St Andrews was founded, by Bishop Roger, to form both a fortress and palace for the Bishops of St Andrews.

1204 The town of Ayr was granted a Charter by William I.

1205 Reginald, Lord of the Isles and son of Somerled, established a Benedicine community on Iona.

1206 Urquhart Castle, on the shores of Loch Ness, was built as a royal fortress.

1207 The lands of Golspie in Sutherland were obtained by a Flemish trader whose descendents subsequently built Dunrobin Castle.

1208 The destruction by the Scots of King John of England's new castle at Tweedmouth.

1209 William I of Scotland, supported in an alliance with France, agreed peace at the Treaty of Norham with England. Two of William's daughters were to be married to King John's sons and 15,000 Scots merks paid to England.

1210 Birth of Robert Bruce of Annandale, grandfather of Robert the Bruce.

1211 A rising against the crown occurred, led by Guthred, son of Donald MacWilliam.

1212 William's son, Alexander, was promised in marriage to John of England's two-year-old daughter, Joan.

1212 Alexander promised in marriage to King John's two year old daughter

1213 The Merchant Guild was established in Dundee, for the purpose of trading in wool, hides and sheepskins.

1214 William I, (The Lion) died and his only son, Alexander II, became King of Scotland, at the age of 16.

1215 Alexander II supported the English barons in their struggle against King John. In the Magna Carta, John agreed along with the barons, to award the northern counties as an 'Earldom' to Alexander.

1216 The Pope released King John of England from his promises in the Magna Carta, and John sent an army north to burn and plunder in Lothian. Alexander's troops marched south to join up with King Louis of France's troops, taking Carlisle on the way.

1217 Settlement terms agreed with England. The Scots gave up Carlisle.

1218 The Culross Abbey in Fife was founded by Earl Malcolm as a Cistercian monastery.

1219 The Cistercian Abbey of St Mary was founded by William Comyn, Earl of Buchan, near to the ruins of the Abbey of Deer, in Aberdeenshire.

1220 The Earl de Maccuswell was appointed Sheriff of Peebles.

1221 Alexander II married Joanna, sister of Henry III, then went off to subjugate Cowal and Kintyre.

1222 Alexander II ordered the hands and feet of 80 men, who had been present at the murder of Bishop Adam of Caithness, to be cut off.

1223 Gilbert, the Archdeacon of Moray, was made Bishop of Caithness. He designed the Cathedral of Dornoch and built St Peter's Church in Thurso.

1224 The Cathedral of the Bishop of Moray was chartered to Elgin, thereby replacing Spynie as the Cathedral of the See of Moray.

1225 The island of 'Clarinch' on Loch Lomond, was granted to Absalon of Buchannan by the Earl of Lennox. The name of the island became the war cry of the Clan Buchanan.

1226 The founding of Balmerino Abbey in Fife, by Ermengarde, widow of William I.

1227 Abbey founded near Edderton, Ross and Cromarty, on the Dornoch Firth, by Farquhar, Earl of Ross.

1228 A rising in Badenoch and Lochaber against Alexander II, was put down.

1229 Kildrummy Castle, near Alford, Aberdeenshire, was founded by the Earl of Mar on the instructions of Alexander II.

1230 A Viking force unsuccessfully besieged Rothesay Castle on the Isle of Bute.

1231 Blackfriars Monastry in Perth was founded by Alexander II. It was the scene of the murder of James I (see 1436).

1232 The Valliscaulian Order founded a Priory at Beauly in Inverness-shire.

1233 Marriage of Devorguilla, daughter of Alan, Lord of Galloway, to John Balliol. As well as holding land in Galloway, Aberdeenshire and Angus, she was to transmit a claim to the throne to her son, John.

1234 Henry III broke the Treaty of 1209. Alexander II of Scotland demanded the northern Earldom of the three counties of England, and the return of the 15,000 Scots merks paid under the Treaty.

1235 An alliance was drawn up by Alexander II, Llewelyn of North Wales and some discontented English lords and barons, against Henry III of England.

1236 Meeting of Alexander II and Henry III in York, where they discussed relations between the two countries.

1237 The Treaty of York between Alexander II and Henry III, was arranged through Pope Gregory IX. As a result Alexander abandoned his claim to the counties of Northumberland, Cumberland and Westmorland, but received land in the northern English counties valued at £200 income per year.

1238 Death of Olaf the Black, King of the Isles, who had been imprisoned by William I in 1208. He contested the Isles crown with his brother, Reginald, whom he finally defeated at Dingwall in 1230.

1239 Marriage, in Roxburgh Castle, of Alexander II to Marie de Coucy, daughter of the Baron of Coucy in Picardy. After Alexander's death in 1249, she returned to France in 1251 and married the son of the King of Jerusalem.

1240 Birth of Robert Wishart, who in 1271, was appointed Bishop of Glasgow. In 1305 he became Bruce's chief advisor. He was captured in 1306 and in 1308 sent to Avignon for papal judgement. He died in 1316.

1241 The birth of the only son of Alexander II and Marie de Coucy, at Roxburgh. He was inaugurated as Alexander III at Scone in 1249, when eight years of age.

1242 Consecration by David de Bernham, Bishop of St Andrews, of the Parish of Abdie, south-east of Newburgh.

1243 The High Kirk of Edinburgh was dedicated to St Giles, 'Egidius'. (A Greek hermit who moved to Provence in the 6th century.)

1244 Forces under Alexander II and Henry III faced up to one another at the border. At a Treaty in Newcastle, Alexander promised not to make any more alliances with France and Henry agreed the marriage of his daughter Margaret to Alexander's son, Alexander III.

1245 Death of St Gilbert of Moray at Dornoch Cathedral; the last Scotsman to be canonised before the Reformation.

1246 The Dominican Order established a monastery on the east side of the High Street, Glasgow. It is now Blackfriars' Street.

1247 Alexander II granted tenancy to the Abbey of Lindores, near Broughty Ferry.

1248   Ewen, of the Clan MacDougall, was invested as 'King of Scots', by Haakon IV of Norway.

1249   Alexander II arrived at the Island of Kerrera, off Oban, at the head of a fleet to subdue the Isles, but took ill and died in Horseshoe Bay. He was succeeded by his only son, Alexander III.

1250   Alexander III gave the monks of Paisley the right to construct a fish farm, on the River Leven.

1251   Marriage, at York, of Alexander III (aged 10) and Margaret (aged 11), daughter of Henry III of England.

1252   The harpist, Adam of Lennox, became the Abbot of Balmerino, Fife.

1253   A priory was established in Blantyre, Lanarkshire, by Augustians from Jedburgh.

1254   Gamline was appointed Chancellor of Scotland. He became Bishop of St Andrews the following year.

1255 The monopoly of power by the family of Comyns caused problems. King Henry of England came to the Border on the basis that the Scottish queen, his daughter, was not being treated honourably. As a result, a Council of Regency was appointed and the Comyns banished from all office.

1256 The Maison Dieu Almshouse was founded in Brechin, Angus.

1257 The Comyns and other Scottish lords, allegedly 'fearing the dishonour of the King and the Kingdom', siezed the king and assembled an army to oppose Henry III and his supporters in Scotland.

1258 Council appointed which contained representitives from all parties to rule between 1259 and 1261, until the King, Alexander III, came of age.

1259 Death of Matthew Paris, the mapmaker of Scotland.

1260 Red Dugald MacSween captured the west-coast land as far south as Skipness.

1261 The Cross Kirk in Peebles was founded by Alexander III.

1262 The Scots invaded the Isle of Skye.

1263 Battle of Largs. Forces of King Haakon were repelled by the Scots under Alexander III.

1264 Birth of Alexander, Prince of Scotland. He was the elder son of Alexander III and was to marry Margaret of Flanders. He left no heirs.

1265   Birth of William Lamberton, who became Bishop of St Andrews, and crowned Bruce at his Coronation in 1306.

1266   Scotland acquired the Western Isles and the Isle of Man from Norway under the Treaty of Perth. The payment was 4,000 Scots merks and an annual rent of 100 merks. (The Scots merk was worth two-thirds of an English pound).

1267   Work commenced on Blair Castle, Blair Atholl, Perthshire, by master builder, John Comyn of Badenoch. It is the ancient seat of the Dukes of Atholl.

1268   A massive wall was built around Skipness Castle in Kintyre, by the Earl of Menteith.

1269   A Carmelite Friary was founded in Berwick.

1270   Birth of Sir William Wallace, second son of Sir Malcolm Wallace of Elderslie, Renfrewshire.

1271   The hospital and chapel of St Leonard was built onto Holyrood Abbey, Edinburgh.

1272 The 'Hammer of the Scots', Edward I, succeeded his father, Henry III, to the throne of England.

1273 Sweetheart Abbey, five miles south of Dumfries in Kirkcudbrightshire, was founded by Devorgilla Balliol, who preserved her husband's heart there in an ivory casket. He had died in 1268.

1274 Birth at Turnberry, of Robert, eldest son of Robert Bruce of Annandale and Marjorie, Countess of Carrick. He became Robert I, 'the Bruce'.

1275 The inhabitants of the Isle of Man were defeated by Scottish forces.

1276 Birth of Edward Bruce, the younger brother of Robert the Bruce. He became King of Ireland but was killed at Dundalk in 1318.

1277 Birth of Gilbert, the future Earl of Angus. He fought against Bruce at Bannockburn, was captured and stripped of his Scottish lands.

1278 Robert Bruce, the father of Robert I, went on a second crusade to the Holy Land. (He first went in 1270 with Edmund, the youngest son of Henry III).

1279 Death of Leod, first head of the 'MacLeod' Clan, and of Viking descent. His lands in Lewis and Harris, and also Dunvegan in Skye, were divided amongst his sons.

1280 The introduction of halfpennies and farthings into Scotland.

1281 Alexander III's daughter, Margaret, married King Haakon's grandson, Eric II of Norway.

1282 Devorgilla, wife of John Balliol, sealed the Charter of Oxford's Balliol College at Buittle Castle, Dalbeattie, Kirkcudbrightshire.

1283 The death of Alexander III's daughter, Margaret, whilst giving birth to a daughter, who was briefly to become Queen of Scotland as Margaret, 'Maid of Norway'.

1284 The king's only son, Alexander, aged 20, died. Margaret, the 'Maid of Norway' and infant granddaughter of Alexander III was acknowledged as heir to the throne, provided the king had no further children.

1285 Second marriage of Alexander III; to Yolande of Dreux, the daughter of Robert IV. The wedding feast was held in Jedburgh.

1286 Alexander III was killed at Kinghorn, near Burntisland in Fife. His horse stumbled and threw him over a cliff. (A monument erected in 1887 marks the spot.) Margaret, age three, was declared Queen.

1287 Death of Thomas of Ercildoune, 'The Rhymer', a Border laird who is reported to have written the *Romance of Sir Tristren*.

1287 Death of Thomas 'The Rhymer'

1288 An abbey was built near the village of Hill of Fearn, near Nigg in Ross and Cromarty. The chapel of the abbey is now incorporated into the parish church.

1289 The Castle of Dundee was established. It was demolished by 1314.

1290 Margaret, the 'maid of Norway', died on her way to Scotland in the company of ambassador, Sir David Wemyss. She was buried in Bergen.

1291 Claim to the throne by John Balliol, but contested by a dozen rivals, 'The Competitors', including Robert the Bruce.

1292 John Balliol selected as King of Scotland by Edward I and crowned at Scone on St Andrew's Day. He was the last king to be enthroned in Scotland on the Stone of Destiny.

1293 First records of the Scottish Parliament, which had started in 1201. Unlike England, they met as a single body in one chamber and not the 'three estates', clergy, nobility and burgesses. It met until the Act of Union in 1707.

1294 Sir Colin Campbell, Chief of the Campbells, was killed in a skirmish with MacDougall, Lord of the Isles, in Argyll.

1295 A Treaty was drawn up between King John Balliol and Philip IV ('The Fair') of France. This was the start of the 'Auld Alliance' between Scotland and France.

1296 Edward I removed the Stone of Scone from Scone Abbey to Westminster Abbey. (See also 1996).

1297 The stunning victory at Stirling Bridge by William Wallace, established him as the leader of the Scottish resistance movement. The Scottish forces under Wallace and Andrew Murray attacked the English when half had come over the narrow wooden bridge of Stirling. English losses were enormous. Their leader, Cressingham, was killed and his skin distributed amongst the Scots as souvenirs.

1298 William Wallace defeated at Falkirk by Edward I ('Longshanks'). Wallace resigned his post of Guardian of Scotland. (A second Battle of Falkirk took place in 1746 between the Jacobites of Prince Charles Edward's army and government troops under General Hawley.

1299 David de Moravia was appointed Bishop of Moray. He was excommunicated in 1306 for his support of Robert the Bruce.

14TH CENTURY

1300 The siege of Caerlaverock Castle, near Dumfries, by an army led by Edward I of England. Eventually the occupiers, the Maxwells, surrendered.

1301 Death of 'Black Comyn', the son of the 'Red Comyn'.

1302 Robert the Bruce was offered a truce, by Edward I.

1303 Sir Thomas Maule held out for three weeks in Brechin Castle, against the army of Edward I.

1304 Death of Robert Bruce. The future Robert I, 7th Lord of Annandale, succeeded his father.

1305 William Wallace was captured at Robroyston, Glasgow and imprisoned at Dumbarton Castle, before being taken to London for execution. One of the two summits on the castle rock is called Wallace's Seat.

1306 Robert the Bruce crowned King of Scotland at Scone. (He was crowned again because Isabella, Countess of Buchan, was missing at the first ceremony).

1307 Victory by Robert the Bruce over English forces at Glentrool, Galloway.

1308 Robert the Bruce defeated the Earl of Buchan at the Battle of Inverurie, Oldmeldrum, Aberdeenshire.

1309 John MacDougall of Lorne held the Pass of Brander in Argyll for Edward II, but was defeated by Robert the Bruce and the Black Douglas, who charged from the slopes of Ben Cruachan into the battle.

1310 Declarations in favour of Robert the Bruce were issued by the provincial clergy at Dundee.

1311 Bernard of Linton, Chancellor to Robert the Bruce, was appointed 'Vicar' of Glasgow.

1312 Robert the Bruce attempted to take the town of Berwick-upon-Tweed, but his force's presence was betrayed by a dog barking.

1313 Edinburgh Castle was recaptured from the English by Sir Thomas Randolph and William Francis, who scaled the rock at night with only 30 men.

1314 The Battle of Bannockburn. The decisive battle in the Wars of Independence. England under Edward II had 16,000 infantry, 2,500 mounted knights and a 20-mile supply train. Robert the Bruce had 6,000 spearmen, some archers and 500 light horse troops. The English were cut down on the banks of the Bannock Burn by the Scottish spearmen to secure Scottish nationhood.

1315 Marjorie Bruce, Robert Bruce's only child from his first marriage, married Walter Stewart, (hence the Stewart succession). Her tomb is in Paisley Abbey.

1316 The town of Bathgate, West Lothian, was given by Robert the Bruce to Walter the High Steward.

1317 The death of Robert the Bruce's brother-in-law, Neil Campbell.

1318 Consecration of the new Cathedral at St Andrews by Bishop Lamberton. Robert the Bruce rode up the central aisle on his horse during the ceremony.

1319 Scotland retained Berwick following an attack by the English. John Crab of Aberdeen was the military architect who devised the catapults and fortifications for its defence.

1320 The Declaration of Arbroath, sometimes called the Declaration of Independence. It was 'sealed' by eight earls and 31 barons and penned by the Abbot of Arbroath, Bernard of Linton. The Declaration, justifying Scottish Independence, was sent to Pope John XXII who had sympathised with English claims to Scotland.

1321 Lands of Tullibardine, near Auchterarder, granted to the Murray family. It is recorded that the length and breadth of James IV's battleship, the *Great Michael*, was planted in hawthorne at Tullibardine, by the shipwright who helped make her.

1322 Victory by Robert the Bruce against Edward II at the Battle of Byland Abbey, in Yorkshire.

1323 Robert the Bruce overcame papal opposition and was recognised as the King of Scotland, mainly through the efforts of Scotland's envoy in Italy, Thomas Randolph, the Earl of Moray.

1324 Birth of David II, son of Robert the Bruce and his queen, Elizabeth de Burgh.

1325 Tarbert Castle, at the north end of the Kintyre peninsula, was strengthened under the direction of Robert the Bruce.

1326 The 'Auld Alliance' renewed at the Treaty of Corbeil, and ratified at Stirling.

1327 The death of Elizabeth de Burgh of Ulster, second wife of Robert.

1328 At the Treaty of Northampton, Edward III agreed to give up all colonial ambitions and recognised the kingship of Bruce and the independence of Scotland. This ended the 30 years of the Wars of Independence.

1329 Death of Robert Bruce, from leprosy, at Cardross Castle near the mouth of the River Leven. His embalmed heart was taken on an abortive journey to the Holy Land, but eventually was buried at Melrose Abbey.

1330 Death of 'Good Sir James' Douglas, Earl of Douglas, fighting the Moors in Spain, on his way to the Holy Land with the heart of Robert the Bruce.

1331 David II, son of Robert the Bruce, crowned at Scone at the age of seven. A small sceptre was designed for him to bear.

1331 David II crowned
aged seven.

1332 Battle of Annan when troops under Sir Archibald Douglas launched a dawn attack on Balliol's camp. The half-dressed Balliol was forced to leap onto his horse and make a dash for the border…'one leg booted and the other bare'.

1333 Scotland, under Douglas, defeated at the Battle of Halidon Hill; from their vantage point on the hilltop the English archers mowed down the climbing Scots with wave after wave of arrows.

1334 David II and his young Queen Joanna, age 13, sailed from Dumbarton Castle, to join Philip VI in France.

1335 The Battle of Culblean on Culblean Hill near Dinnet, Aberdeenshire, when forces under Moray surprised and defeated an army under the Earl of Atholl, who had been beseiging Kildrummy.

1336 An unsuccessful attempt by Andrew de Moray to wrest Dunnottar Castle, near Stonehaven, from the English.

1337 The Castle of Bothwell was taken by troops under Sir Andrew Murray.

1338 A resolute and successful defence of Dunbar Castle was organised by Agnes, Countess of Dunbar, known as 'Black Agnes' because of her complexion and dark hair. Forces for the English King, Edward III, pounded the castle with cannons over a six-month period. It is said she went around clearing up any debris when cannon balls hit parts of the castle.

1338   Black Agnes
        at the siege of Dunbar

1339 Edward III's fortresses in Scotland were all
recaptured by the Scots following his invasion of
France and the start of the Hundred Years' War.

1340 Birth of the 1st Duke of Albany, Robert Stewart,
the younger brother of Robert III. Seen as devious,
cynical and politically astute, he, in effect, ruled
Scotland for 14 years. He died at the age of 80.

1341 David II and his queen, Joanna, returned from
exile in France and landed at Inverbervie after a
very stormy passage.

1342 Sir William Douglas, Lord of Liddesdale plotted
the death of Alexander Ramsay, who had previously
had Teviotdale and Roxburgh given to him by David
II.

1343 The birth of Euphemia, Countess of Ross, daughter
of William Earl of Ross. She married Sir Walter
Leslie and later, Alexander Stewart.

1344 Birth of Alexander Stewart, the Earl of Buchan, better remembered as the 'Wolf of Badenoch'. In 1390, after being censured by the Bishop of Moray for his adultery, The 'Wolf' razed the town of Forres and the Cathedral of Elgin.

1345 Bishop Rae of Glasgow sanctioned the first stone bridge across the Clyde.

1346 David II was defeated by forces led by the Archishop of York at Neville's Cross. He was taken to London as a prisoner. (See 1357).

1347 Robert II married Elizabeth Mure of Rowallan, by whom he already had several children.

1348 Robert Stewart, the Governor of Scotland, planned a rebellion with the Earl of Douglas. (It did not happen due to the epidemic of 1349).

Sorry - REBELLION CANCELLED DUE TO SICKNESS

1349 The Black Death plague reached Scotland.
Tens of thousands died.

1350 John Kennedy of Dunure, north of Culzean,
Ayrshire, received the Earldom of Cassillis.

1351 The chantry chapel of the parish church of Straiton,
in Ayrshire, was founded.

1352 The Hospital of St John the Baptist was built in
Arbroath.

1353 Sir William Douglas of Liddesdale, was murdered
in a family quarrel.

1354 Scottish forces were defeated near Berwick.

1355 A Scottish force defeated an English army at the
Battle of Nesbit, just south of Berwick. (A further
battle also took place in Nesbit in 1402, when the
Scots were defeated).

1356 Edward Balliol, son of John Balliol was dismissed
by Edward III with a pension during the year of
'Burnt Candlemas', Edward III's last campaign.
He left behind a trail of smouldering castles.

1357 David II returned to the kingdom, following
payment of ransom under the Treaty of Berwick.

1358 The introduction of new coins. Large silver groats
(initially fourpence), half-groats (twopence) and the
'noble', the first gold coin.

1359 Dundee created a sheriffdom and allowed to send
representatives to the Scottish Parliament.

1360 The grounds of Clackmannan Tower Castle in Clackmannanshire, were granted by David II to a Robert Bruce (an illegitimate grandson of Robert I).

1361 The reoccurrence of the Black Death in Scotland.

1362 Birth of Murdoch Stewart, 2nd Duke of Albany. He was taken prisoner in 1402 by the English and ransomed in 1415. Became the Duke of Albany and the Regent of Scotland in 1420, but did not have a good relationship with James I when the King returned from imprisonment in England (see 1425).

1363 Lands were granted in Alloa, to the Erskines of Mar.

1364 David II granted Royal Burghs a monopoly on foreign trade; normally with the Low Countries and Baltic States.

1365 Robert III first met his future bride, Annabella Dummond, at Perth.

1366 David's Tower in Edinburgh Castle was begun by David II and completed some ten years later. Its lower storeys were rediscovered in 1912.

1367 Annabella Drummond, daughter of Sir John Drummond of Stobhall,Perthshire married Robert III. She subsequently gave birth to seven children, including James I.

1368 From this year onwards, the heir to the throne had included in their titles, 'the Earldom of Carrick'.

1369 The Town Hall (Praetorium) of Edinburgh was erected near the Mercat Cross. It was burnt by Richard II in 1385.

1370 The parish church in St Monans, Fife, built on the instructions of David II, was completed and opened. It was restored in 1826.

1371 Death of David II. He was succeeded by his nephew Robert Stewart, age 55, son of Walter, Robert Bruce's son-in-law.

1372 Birth of Archibald Douglas, 4th Earl of Douglas. He was called 'The Tyneman' (the loser) after a series of defeats.

1373 Birth of Laurence of Lindores, the sinister figure from St Andrews, who for over 30 years was the Inquisitor of Heretical Pravity.

THE INQUISITOR OF HERETICAL PRAVITY

1374 Sir Simon Preston of Craigmillar Castle, near Duddingston, received a Charter of Barony from Robert II.

1375 Cairnbulg Castle, Aberdeenshire, acquired by the Frasers of Philorth. (They subsequently founded Fraserburgh).

1376 A naval battle was fought off Inchture, between ships belonging to Robert II and English pirates.

1377 The town of Berwick was held by seven Scots, for eight days, against English forces.

1378 The birth of David Stewart, the 1st Duke of Rothesay and son of Robert III. Appointed Lieutenant of the Kingdom in 1398 but arrested three years later by his uncle, Albany. He died in 1402.

1379 The mainland pendicle of the Norse Earldom of Orkney (Caithness) passed to Henry Sinclair.

1380 Birth of John Stewart, the Earl of Buchan. He Chamberlain on Albany's behalf in 1408; was one of the Commanders on the Franco-Scottish side at the defeat of the English army at Anjou but was killed in the subsequent defeat by the English at Verneuil.

1381 Outbreak of Black Death plague in the central belt of Scotland.

1382 The Battle of Benrig at which the Scots, under the Earl of Dunbar, defeated English forces under the Baron of Greystoke. (The English had been on their way to occupy Roxburgh Castle.)

1383 John of Fordun, a chronicler from Aberdeen, wrote a latin history of medieval history, up to 1383. He died in 1387.

1384 The Scots were given Berwick through the corruption of the Deputy-Governor. He retook the town some months later.

1385 The rebuilt Dryburgh Abbey, St Boswells, Roxburghshire and St Giles, Edinburgh, were burnt down by Richard II.

1386 Death of Ranald, eldest surviving son of 'Good' John of Isla, 1st Lord of the Isles and High Chief of the Clan Donald, at Castle Tioram in Moidart.

1387 John, the 1st MacDonald Lord of the Isles, died at Ardtornish Castle, Morvern, Argyll.

1388 Battle of Otterburn between forces under Sir Henry Peroy, the celebrated Hotspur, and James, the Earl of Douglas. After an all-night battle, victory went to the Scots. Douglas who had been mortally wounded at the start of the battle, requested that he be hidden in a bush so that none of the English would know. This gave rise to the phrase, 'a dead man won the field'.

1389 Robert II granted the Earldom of Angus to George Douglas.

1390 Robert II died in Ayr and his eldest son, Robert III, started his reign, despite having been badly disabled in a riding accident in 1388.

1391 Robert III was ill with severe depression and unable to govern. His brother, Robert, Earl of Fife (Albany), assumed the title, Governor of the Realm.

1392 Donald, Lord of the Isles, gave lands in Mull and Tiree to his brother-in-law, Lachan MacLean of Duart.

1393 Robert III declared himself well and fit to reign and took over control of government.

1394 Birth at Dunfermline Monastery of the future James I, who was second son of Robert III and Queen Annabella. After the eldest son, David, was murdered, James was sent to France for safety. (See 1406).

1395 Death of John Barbour, the poet. He was a member of the Royal Household and is remembered for his lengthy poem *Romance of the Brus*, written in 1375 about the exploits of Robert I.

1396 Clan battle at North Inch, Perth, between 30 picked gladiators of the Clan Chattan (Mackintosh) and the Clan Kay (MacKay). Twenty-nine Kays and 19 Chattans were killed.

1397 Foundations laid of Newark Castle, on the River Yarrow, near Selkirk. In 1645 over a hundred defeated Royalists took refuge in the castle before being brutally massacred by the Covenanters. (NB: there are four Newark Castles in Scotland).

1398 Robert III created his son, David, as the first Scottish Duke (Rothesay) and Alba, the former name for Scotland, was relegated to the title of a Royal Dukedom.

1399 Robert III, whose health had deteriorated, handed over authority to both his younger brother, the Duke of Albany and his eldest son, David, Duke of Rothesay.

15TH CENTURY

1400 Unsuccessful seige of Edinburgh Castle by forces under Henry IV, after the Scots ignored his order that Robert III and the Scottish nobility, pay homage to him.

1401 Donald Dubh was appointed First Chief of the Cameron Clan. Cam-shron, according to Gaelic genealogical theory, means 'crooked nose'.

1402 Start of the regency of the Duke of Albany after he had imprisoned Robert III's son, the Duke of Rothesay, in prison and starved him to death.

1403 The Earl of Douglas agreed to a ransom for his freedom, by fighting for Hotspur against King Henry IV of England, at Shewsbury.

1404 Robert III granted a perpetual free Royal Charter to the monks of Crossraguel Abbey, Maybole, Ayrshire and gave them the privilege of minting their own coins, brewing their own ale and fishing in the River Girvan.

1405 Marriage of Elizabeth Gordon and Alexander Seton, bringing together the lands of Strathbogie, Aboyne, Glenmuick and Glentanar.

1406   Death of Robert III. James, heir to Robert III, was captured by pirates on the way to France and handed over to Henry IV of England. He was imprisoned for 17 years. Albany took control of Scotland.

1407   John Resby, a follower of John Wycliffe, the Bible translator, was martyred at Perth.

1408   Severe storms on east coast damaged the Cathedral of St Andrews.

1409   A Treaty of Accommodation was agreed between Archibald, the fourth Earl of Douglas, and Albany.

1410   Laigh Park in Kilmarnock was designed and laid out.

1411   Battle of Red Harlaw two miles north-west of Inverurie, between Donald, second Lord of the Isles and the Scots Government led by the Earl of Mar.

1412   University of St Andrews founded by Bishop Henry Wardlaw, its first Chancellor. It was the first university in Scotland.

1413   St Leonards Chapel in St Andrews built as a parish church. It still belongs to the University.

1414   Henry Ogilvy, Master of Arts of the Universities of Paris and St Andrews, returned to St Andrews after his pilgrimage to Benedicts Court in Spain.

1415   Death of John Dhu, from whose sons the MacGregors of Roro and Glengyle in Perthshire, and Brackly in Argyll, are descended.

1416 Dundas Castle near Queensferry, licensed by Robert, Duke of Albany.

1417 Major outbreak of the plague, the Black Death, throughout Scotland.

1418 Death of Henry Sinclair, the Earl of Orkney, who was also Admiral of Scotland. He had sailed with James I when he was captured by the English. (See 1406).

1419 The Duke of Albany, Regent of Scotland, sent a contingent to France to fight for the Dauphin against Henry V.

1420 Death of the first Duke of Albany. His son Murdach inherited his power until James was freed by England in 1424.

1421 Archibald, son of the 4th Earl of Douglas, headed a Scottish force at Bauge in France, on the side of the Dauphin Charles against the English.

1422 The Scottish Regent made an abortive attempt to take Berwick.

1423 Donald of Harlaw's son, Alexander, became Lord of the Isles. He made peace with King James I, and was appointed Royal Justiciar for Scotland north of the River Forth.

1424 Archibald, the 4th Earl of Douglas, led an army of 10,000 to France to fight for the Dauphin Charles against the English. He was killed at the Battle of Verneuil.

1425 Albany's son, Murdoch, the second Duke of Albany, who had been Regent since 1420, was beheaded along with his two sons, Walter and Alexander, plus his father-in-law, the Earl of Lennox; the executions took place in front of Stirling Castle.

1426 Reform in judicial matters with an act prescribing that the Chancellor and 'discreet persons' from the estates, should hear 'causes and complaints'.

1427 Parliament held in Inverness. James I ordered that 50 highland chiefs be imprisoned.

1428 James I again summoned the Highland Chiefs to Inverness where Alexander, Lord of the Isles was taken into temporary custody.

1429 Kenneth, the 6th MacKenzie Chief, accepted Margaret MacDonald, a daughter of the Lord of the Isles as his bride. However, finding her blind in one eye, he sent her back home with a horse, a groom and a dog, all also blind in one eye. The result was a ferocious battle between the clans, fought near Strathpeffer, in Ross and Cromarty.

1430 The building of Borthwick Castle near Gorebridge, Midlothian started by Sir William Borthwick. It boasts the tallest tower house in Scotland and is well-preserved to this day.

1431 The four-storey tower near Alloa was built by Sir James Schaw (who was later implicated in the murder of James III).

1432 James I placed St Andrews University under his personal protection, exempting its members from all taxation.

1433 The burning of Paul Craw, the first heretic to be martyred in Scotland. (In Market Street, St Andrews.)

1434 Forfeiture of the Castle of Dunbar, in East Lothian, home of the Earls of Dunbar and March, to James I.

1435 Death of Alexander Stewart, son of the 'Wolf of Badenoch'. He had fought at the Battle of Harlaw in 1411.

1436 Following a plot by Sir Robert Stewart, James I was murdered by intruders in the cellar at Perth's Blackfriars Monastry. One of the Queen's ladies (Kate Bar-Lass) put her arm through the door staples to delay the intruders.

1437 James II, the six-year-old heir to the throne was crowned at Holyrood. (He was called 'Fiery Face' because of an unusual birthmark). Archibald, 5th Earl of Douglas, was appointed Regent.

1438 The Berwick Bounds, between the town and the Border, were established.

1439 Death of the Regent, Archibald, 5th Earl of Douglas.

1440 The 'Black Dinner' in Edinburgh Castle when the young 6th Earl of Douglas and his younger brother were, whilst having dinner with the boy King James II, dragged out and murdered. It is said a black bull's head was placed on the dinner table.

1441 Work on St Mary's Episcopal Church in Queensferry was started when James Dundas, of Dundas Castle, granted the White Friar lands.

1442 Collegiate Church, founded by Sir Duncan Campbell of Lochow, at Kilmun on the Holy Loch. It was dedicated to St Mundus, a disciple of St Columba.

1443 William, 8th Earl of Douglas, inherited the Earldom from his father, James 'The Gross'.

1444 The Douglases beseiged and stormed Crighton Castle in Midlothian.

1445 Charles VII of France formed the 'Garde Ecossais', an elite corps of 100 Scots guardsmen and 200 archers. In 1525 the 'Garde Ecossais' were caught in a snow storm near the Simplon Pass in the Alps and decided to settle there. Their descendants, known as the 'Lost Clan', are reputedly still in the area.

THE LOST CLAN

1446 The chapel at Tullibardine was built by the Clan Murray.

1447 Greyfriars Monastery built near to the West Bow in Edinburgh. It was a Franciscan Friary started by Dutch monks.

1448 The Battle of Sark was fought on the north bank of the River Sark, which feeds into the Solway, near Gretna. The English forces led by the Earl of Northumberland were beaten by the Scots under the Earl of Ormonde.

1449 James II married Mary of Gueldres, a princess noted for her piety. Her dowry included cannons technically superior to any hardware available in Scotland at that time. (See 1460).

1450 The famous cannon, Mons or 'Muckle Meg', was manufactured in Mons in Flanders. It weighs over five tons and could fire a shot of over 200lbs more than two miles. It now resides in Edinburgh Castle.

1451 Glasgow University founded by Bishop William Turnbull. Among its professors over the centuries were Lord Kelvin and Lord Lister.

1452 William, the 8th Earl of Douglas, was stabbed to death by James II at Stirling Castle. The King then threw the corpse out of a window.

1453 James Douglas, the 9th Earl of Douglas married his brother's widow, the Maid of Galloway.

1454 The massive central tower of Cawdor Castle, Nairnshire, was built by William Thane. The castle was popularised by Shakespeare.

Stirling Castle
1452

1455   The Battle of Arkinholm at which forces, under James II, defeated an army of Douglas supporters under the Earl of Moray (who was killed in the battle).

1456   The Golf Tavern opened at Bruntsfield Links to meet the demands of Royal golfers and their retinue.

1457   James II, outlawed the playing of golf and football in order that citizens concentrate on their archery skills.

1458   The son of Mary, daughter of Robert III and Sir James Kennedy, was created Lord Kennedy.

1457. Football outlawed

1459 Berwick-upon-Tweed given to Scotland by Henry IV of England.

1460 James II killed by an exploding cannon at the siege of Roxburgh Castle; James III became King.

1461 Glasgow University colonised new land in Glasgow along the line of the High Street.

1462 The Treaty of Ardtornish signed at Ardtornish Castle, Morvern, Argyll, by MacDonald, the 4th Lord of the Isles and the Ambassador of Edward IV of England. The Treaty was defied by many of the clans, including the MacDonalds.

1463 Archibald Douglas succeeded to the title of the 5th Earl of Angus. Known as 'Bell the Cat', he drew the short straw to reduce the influence on James III by some of his courtiers, based on the story of 'The mice would fain hang a bell around the cat that preyed on them'. 'Bell the Cat' captured seven courtiers and hung them from Lauder Bridge.

1464 George Gunn became the Warden of Caithness.
It was his son, James, who founded the line of chiefs
of the Clan Gunn.

1465 Birth of Hector Boece, the historian, in Dundee.
He was the Principal of the University of Aberdeen
and in 1527 published his *History of Scotland*.

1466 James III, aged 13, kidnapped from Linlithgow
and carried off to Edinburgh Castle.

1467 The creation of 'The Lords of the Articles' – a group
of nobles who drew up potential legislation for
review by the Scottish Parliament.

1468 Treaty between Scotland and Norway. Orkney
was to become Scottish territory as part of the
dowry in the marriage of Margaret, daughter of
Christian I, King of Denmark, Sweden and Norway,
to James III; also promised was 10,000 florins.

1469 Christian I, unable to pay the 10,000 florins,
paid 2,000 and pledged Shetland for the remaining
8,000.

1470 First use of the thistle on silver coins as a Royal
symbol of Scotland, the motto of the Order of the
Thistle is *Nemo Me Imune Lacessit*, or 'No one
provokes me with impunity'.

1471 Provand's Lordship the oldest surviving dwelling
in Glasgow, built by Bishop Andrew Muirhead as
the Preceptor's House of the Hospital of St
Nicholas.

1472 Orkney and Shetland islands annexed by Scotland, as they were unredeemed pledges in the dowry of James III's bride, Margaret from Denmark.

1473 Sir Alexander Home, the Ambassador Extraordinary to England, was appointed a Lord of Parliament by James III. (Sir Alec Douglas Home, who became Prime Minister in 1963, was a descendent from this same family.)

1474 The Earl of Arran was stripped of his title and his wife forced, by James III, to marry James, the Lord Hamilton.

1475 John, the 4th Lord of the Isles, lost the Earldom of Ross on account of rebellions against the Scottish crown.

1476 Sir John Stewart, the Earl of Lennox, had his earldom revoked. It was restored again in 1488, revoked in 1489 for rebelling against James IV and restored for a third time later the same year.

1477 The cloth market was established by James III in the Lawnmarket, Edinburgh.

1477 Cloth Market
established by
James III

1478 The office of Lord Advocate was established. (The Chief Law Officer of the Crown in Scotland with full discretion over criminal prosecutions.)

1479 James III imprisoned his brother, Alexander, Duke of Albany, in David's Tower, Edinburgh Castle, in order to overcome his rivalry for the throne. His other brother, John, Earl of Mar, died the same year in his bath while being bled.

1480 An English army failed to overthrow the Scottish Garrison in Berwick.

1481 Birth of Donald Dubh, grandson of John, the 4th Lord of the Isles, at the Campbell stronghold of Innis Chunnel on Loch Awe.

1482 The favourites of James II, including Sir Robert Cochrane and William Rodgers, were taken and hanged from Lauder Bridge.

1483 Queen Margaret and her eldest son, James, Duke of Rothesay, left James III to live alone in Edinburgh and moved to Stirling.

1484 An unsuccessful raid on Lochmaben by forces under Alexander Stewart, the 3rd Duke of Albany, the son of James II. He was forced to flee to France.

1485 Lachlann Macmhuirich was designated Chief Gaelic Poet to the Chief of the MacDonalds of Kintyre and Islay.

1486 Kirkwall, capital of Orkney, received a Charter as a Royal Burgh from James III.

1487 Restalrig Collegiate Kirk, near Meadowbank, was founded by James III. (He was killed the following year by forces led by his son, James, after the Battle of Sauchieburn).

1488 Whilst returning from his Coronation at Scone Palace, James IV stopped at Blackford to buy a barrel of ale, for 12 Scots shillings.

1489 The seige of Crookston Castle, near Paisley, when forces under James IV attacked the castle, held by the Stewarts of Darnley.

1490 The Scottish Admiral, Andrew Wood, returned to Leith in triumph after capturing five English vessels in a battle in the North Sea.

1491 Broughty Ferry Castle, with its five-storey tower, was built when Lord Gray of Fowlis procured a Charter of the 'Rock and Fishings' at Broughty.

1492 Glasgow was designated an Archbishopric.

1493 Final confrontation between the King and John, 4th Lord of the Isles, arising over a dispute concerning the Treaty of Ardtornish. As a result the Lordship was again forfeited in perpetuity.

1494 Birth of Cardinal David Beaton in Balfour. He ultimately became Archbishop of Arbroath and was assassinated three months after he had ordered the burning at the stake of George Wishart. (See 1546).

1495 University of Aberdeen founded. It was later named 'Kings' in honour of James IV.

1496   Education legislation was passed in the Scottish
         Parliament, designed to implement some
         compulsory education; it called for the education of
         the eldest sons of ruling barons.

1497   James IV issued a Charter recognising the Chief
         of MacKay as the ruler of the Diocese of Caithness
         and Strathnaver in Sutherland.

1498   Kilkerran Castle, near Cambeltown, Argyll, was
         founded by James IV as part of his policy for the
         pacification of the former lands of the Lord of the
         Isles.

1499   The MacKay Clan led by Angus MacKay from
         Strathnaver, invaded Ross but was overpowered by
         the Rosses. They found sanctuary in the Tabat Old
         Church at Portmahomack, but the Rosses set fire to
         the crypt and all the MacKays were burned to
         death.

16TH CENTURY

1500 Foundation of the Castle of Clunie, which stands on an island in Loch Clunie, near Blairgowrie. It was the childhood home of James (The Admirable) Crichton.

1501 Donald Dubh was rescued from the Campbell stronghold of Innis Chunnell on Loch Awe, by the MacDonalds of Glencoe.

1502 Margaret Drummond, the mistress of James IV, was poisoned at Drummond Castle along with her two sisters, Euphemia and Sibilla. It is assumed that she was seen as an obstacle to the King's marriage to Margaret Tudor and was therefore disposed of; the three sisters are buried at Dunblane Cathedral.

1503 James IV married Margaret Tudor, age 13, daughter of Henry VII of England. (The marriage of 'the Thistle and the Rose').

1504 A golf challenge match was played in Edinburgh between the Earl of Bothwell and James IV. It was reputedly won by the Earl.

1505 The Town Council of Edinburgh granted its Charter of Privileges to the Barber Surgeons, the forerunner of the Royal College of Surgeons.

BARBER · SURGEON

1506 The keel was laid of the *Great Michael*. It took
five years to construct at the Royal Dockyard of
Newhaven. She was designed as a ship of war for
James IV's new navy, displaced approx 1,000 tons
and had a crew of 295 men.

1507 Andrew Myllar and Walter Chepman set up the
first printing press in Scotland, under the terms of a
Royal Patent granted by James IV. The firm in the
Southgait, now the Cowgate of Edinburgh, printed
lawbooks, Acts of Parliament and poetry.

1508 Death of Robert Blackadder, Archbishop of
Glasgow, whilst on a pilgrimage to Jerusalem.

1509 David, the 3rd Lord Kennedy, was created Earl
of Cassillis. the family seat being Cassillis House,
near Maybole, Ayrshire.

1510 Birth of John Erskine, the 1st Earl of Mar, who
held various posts including Keeper of Edinburgh
Castle, Captaincy of Stirling Castle, Custodian of
the Child Prince (James VI), and Regent in 1571.

1511 Death of Andrew Barton, the Scottish privateer
in an encounter with a force under Sir Edward

Howard. Sir Edward had been sent after him by
Henry VIII, due to his ongoing successes against
English vessels.

1512 The 'Auld Alliance' reinforced by the presentation
of a 35-gun warship to James IV by the French
Ambassador, De La Motte.

1513 Battle of Flodden Field, in Northumberland.
James IV and most of his nobles were killed. The
English army did not press home their advantage by
invading Scotland; and James V was subsequently
crowned King (aged 17 months).

1514 A group of youths from Hawick, Roxburghshire,
fell upon a troop of English soldiers from Hexham,
camped near Hornshole. They captured and
carried home the 'Hexham Pennant'. Now
commemorated each year by Hawick's Common
Riding.

1515 Margaret Tudor, the widow of James IV, married
Archibald Douglas, 6th Earl of Angus. (They had
one daughter, Margaret, who became the mother of
Lord Darnley). Margaret Tudor divorced Angus in
1526 and married Lord Methven.

1516 Building started on the Auld Kirk of Alloway,
Ayrshire; later to feature in Burns, *Tam o' Shanter*.

1517 Auchtermuchty in Fife was created a Royal Burgh.

1518 A Scottish Bishop was appointed to the great Abbey
of Constance, which had been founded by Irish
monks in 1142.

1519 John MacGregor of Brackly in Argyll was appointed Chief of the Clan Gregor.

1520 The incident of 'Cleanse the Causeway' in Edinburgh's High Street when onlookers had to clear up a bloody mess after a violent street fight. The fight, between the Hamiltons and the Douglases, resulted in the former being chased out of Edinburgh.

1521 'Bruce of Auchebowie's House' was built in St John Street, Stirling.

1522 The 1st Earl of Arran, James Hamilton, who had to flee to France from the 6th Earl of Angus in 1520, returned to Edinburgh and was restored to the Regency Council.

1523 Jedburgh Castle torched by forces under the Earl of Surrey, who had drawn up a plan to create a 12-mile deep 'no man's land' inside the Scottish Border.

1524 Death of Alexander Gordon, the 3rd Earl of Huntly. He was in joint command of the Scots Vanguard at Flodden in 1513; he survived the battle and went on to become a member of the Commission of Regency, during Albany's absence in France.

1525 John Hamilton, the son of the 1st Earl of Arran, was appointed Commendator of Paisley. He became Archbishop of St Andrews in 1547.

1526 The cold-blooded murder took place of John Stewart, Earl of Lennox, by the fiery but talented architect, Sir James Hamilton. No action was taken. He was however beheaded in 1540 for treason.

1527 The Bridge of Dee in Aberdeen was completed.

1528 Patrick Hamilton burned as a heretic at St Andrews on the orders of James Beaton, Archbishop of St Andrews, and a jury of ecclesiastical dignitaries.

1529 The capture and hanging of Johnnie Armstrong, the Border Reiver, at Caerlanrig Chapel in Teviotdale.

1530 Death of William Dunbar, the Scottish poet, who became Scottish Laureate. He wrote an allegory *The Thrissil and the Rois* in honour of the wedding of James IV and Margaret Tudor.

1531 Birth of Lord James Stewart, the Earl of Moray and the illegitimate son of James V; he played a major role during Mary's reign and became Regent to the infant James VI.

1532 Foundation of the Court of Session (Court of Justice) by James V, to improve impartiality.

1533 John Major, the historian born in Gleghornie near Haddington in East Lothian, was appointed Provost of St Salvator's College in St Andrews. John Knox was one of his pupils

1534 Birth in Turin of David Rizzio, who when accompanying a diplomatic mission from Savoy to Scotland in 1561, won the attention of Queen Mary and became her confidante and secretary. (See 1566).

1535 James V's tailor, Robert Spittal, was refused passage by the ferryman over the River Teith, in Perthshire because he had forgotten his change. Spittal was so infuriated he had a bridge erected over the river in 1536 to put the ferryman out of business.

1536 Death in France of John Stewart, the 4th Duke of Albany and Governor of Scotland. He was brought up in France and was summoned to Scotland in 1515 as Regent and Governor to the infant James V. He spoke only French and surrendered his Regency in 1524 when the 12-year-old James V was invested as King.

1537 Lady Jane Douglas, wife of the 6th Lord Glamis, was burnt to death on a charge of plotting to kill James V.

1538 Mary of Guise triumphantly entered Edinburgh at the West Port at the western end of the Grassmarket, on her way to St Andrews to marry James V.

1539 The introduction of the first Scottish coins to bear a date; the gold ducat on which King James V appears wearing a flat bonnet. The ducat, worth 40 shillings, was commonly known as a 'bonnet'.

1540 The introduction of a new coin, 'the bawbee', with a value of around sixpence.

1541 Robert Stewart became the Bishop of Dornoch at the age of 19.

1542 Battle of Solway Moss at which forces sent by James V were trapped in the marshes of the Solway Moss by the English. King James V died two weeks after the battle and Mary I became queen, aged six days.

1543 The Scottish Government, at the Treaty of Greenwich, agreed to the betrothal of the 6-month-old Queen Mary to Edward, aged six years, son of Henry VIII. It was repudiated by the Earl of Arran some months later.

1544 The 'Battle of the Shirts', near Kilmonivaig, between the 400 or so Frasers of Lovat and the 700 Clanranald MacDonalds, led by John Moidartach. It was a very hot day and all combatants removed their shirts. The battle from noon till dusk left only four Frasers and eight MacDonalds alive.

1545 Battle of Ancrum Moor when 5,000 English troops, under the control of Sir Ralph Eure, were defeated by an army of just over 2,000 Scots under Archibald Douglas, the 6th Earl of Angus.

1544 'BATTLE OF THE SHIRTS'

1546 George Wishart, originally a school teacher from Montrose, was burned at the stake. Cardinal Beaton was murdered by followers of Wishart three months later.

1547 Seige of St Andrews Castle at which John Knox was captured and sent to France to serve as a galley slave. He spent 19 months as a prisoner rowing in the galleys.

1548 The Treaty of Haddington made France the guarantor of Scottish liberties and installed French troops in Scotland. The young Queen Mary Stuart left Scotland for France.

1549 George Gordon, the 4th Earl of Huntly, received the Earldom of Moray. The Earldom was transferred to Queen Mary's half-brother, Lord James Stewart in 1562.

1550 Archbishops allowed
eight courses only.

1550 Because of food shortages, a law was passed limiting the number of courses at meals; Archbishops allowed eight dishes but Burgesses only three.

1551 Edward IV and Queen Mary decreed Berwick-upon-Tweed a free town, independent of both Scotland and England.

1552 John Knox participated in the revision of the second English Prayer Book.

1553 Introduction of a new coin, the 'testoon' (from *tête*, as it bore the monarch's head).

1554 Mary of Guise was installed as Regent of Scotland.

1555 The 'Bloody Vespers' event when a local feud between two Moray families, the Dunbars and the Inneses, came to a head in Elgin Cathedral.

1556 Start of the ferry at Cramond; it originally sailed to the Dalmeny Estate.

1557 The 'Lords of the Congregation' signed a deed against the proposed marriage of the future Queen Mary and the Dauphin of France. Signitories included the Earl of Argyll, his son Lord Lorne, the Earls of Glencairn, Morton and Eskine of Dun.

1558 John Knox issued his booklet *The First Blast of the Trumpet Against the Monstrous Regiment of Women* in the same year that Elizabeth I became Queen of England; he was refused permission to enter England again.

1559 John Knox returned to Scotland after 12 years exile. He became the ordained Minister of St Giles and the major influence behind the Scottish Reformation.

1560 The death of Mary of Guise.

1561 Mary, Queen of Scots, returned from France to take up the Scottish crown.

1562 Queen Mary watched the execution of Sir John Gordon in the Earl Marischal's Hall (now Marischal Street) in Aberdeen.

1563 Birth of George Heriot, the goldsmith, known as 'Jinglin' Geordie' and portrayed as such in Sir Walter Scott's *The Fortunes of Nigel*. He became rich and famous as goldsmith and money lender to James IV. He bequeathed £23,625 for the foundation of George Heriot's Hospital and School; Heriot Watt University also carries his name.

JOHN KNOX'S STAG NIGHT

1564 John Knox, age 50, married the 17-year-old daughter of Lord Ochiltree.

1565 The 'Chaseabout Raid' was the name given to the rebellion, led by James Stewart, Earl of Moray, against the marriage of Mary Queen of Scots to her cousin, Henry Stewart, Earl of Darnley.

1566 Mary Queen of Scots' secretary, David Rizzio, was murdered in Holyrood Palace. He was born in Turin, and came to Scotland with the Savoy Ambassador. Originally employed by Mary as a singer, then her secretary. His advancement aroused jealousy amongst the nobles.

1567 Darnley, Queen Mary's Consort, was murdered at Kirk o' Field and Mary married Hepburn, the Earl of Bothwell. Mary was then compelled to abdicate in favour of her son, James VI.

1568 Battle of Langside, which took place in the Queen's Park area of Glasgow, when Queen Mary's forces were routed by those of the Regent Moray.

1569 The building of a palace was begun in Birsay, Orkney, for the Stewart Earls.

1570 The 'Roasting' of Allan Stewart, Commendator of Crossragvel Abbey, by the 4th Earl of Cassillis. Stewart was bound to a spit and roasted before the great fire in the 'black vault' of Dundee Castle until he surrendered his lands to the Earl. The Earl was fined £2,000 for the outrage and had to pay his victim a pension. However he retained the lands.

1571 Dumbarton Castle was taken in a daring attack by Thomas Crawford of Jordanhill, after it had held out in favour of Mary.

1572 Death of John Knox, aged 58, thirteen days after his last sermon in St Giles.

1573 Thirty-three-day siege of Edinburgh Castle which was commanded by Sir William Kirkcaldy of Grange. The castle eventually fell.

1574 A castle was built at Kinnaird Head, Fraserburgh by Sir Alexander Fraser of Philorth. It is now a lighthouse.

1575 Robert Stewart, the Earl of Orkney, was imprisoned by the Regent James Douglas, Earl of Morton. He had been trying to sell Orkney to the King of Denmark.

1576 Start of horse racing at Belleisle, Ayrshire. It moved to the present racecourse in Ayr, in 1907.

1577 John Damian jumped from Stirling Castle with wings strapped to his arms, in an unsuccessful attempt to fly. He broke a thigh bone but survived.

1577   John Damian, pioneer airman.

1578   James VI's first Parliament met in the Great Hall
of Stirling Castle.

1579   Death of Henry Balnaves the reformer, who was
sent with John Knox to the French galleys following
the capture of St Andrews Castle (see 1547).

1580   James Douglas, 4th Earl of Morton, was tried in
Edinburgh for his part in the murder of Lord
Darnley. He was beheaded by the 'Maiden'

guillotine, in Edinburgh's Glassmarket the following
year. (The 'Maiden' is now in the Royal Museum of
Scotland in Edinburgh).

1581 The execution of the Regent Morton on a charge
of complicity in the murder of the King's father.
(He too was guillotined by the 'Maiden', which he
himself had introduced into Scotland).

1582 Edinburgh University founded. The oldest non-
ecclesiastical university in Britain, it opened the
following year with 80 students.

1583 Death of James Crichton of Eliock, who as 'The
Admirable Crichton' matriculated at St Andrews in
1570, aged 10. A fine horseman and fencer he was
fluent in 12 languages; travelled from university to
university on the continent amusing himself and
outwitting their best scholars in debate.

1584 The 'Raid of Stirling' when the Earls of Mar, Glamis
and Angus, along with the Lords John and Claude
Hamilton, seized Stirling Castle. James VI then
beseiged the castle whose occupiers fled over the
Border.

1585 A raid took place against James VI at Stirling
Castle, led by the Earls of Bothwell and Home,
aided by William Armstrong, 'Kinmont Willie', the
Border Reiver.

1586 Death of Robert Stewart who had become Bishop
of Caithness at the age of 19. He finished his days
at St Andrews, squandering funds.

1587 Mary Queen of Scots was executed at Fotheringay Castle. Her body was moved to Westminister Abbey in 1612.

1588 The Spanish galleon, *Florida*, part of the Armada, sank in Tobermory Bay, Mull. It was said to be carrying £300,000 worth of gold bullion.

1589 Marriage of Princess Anne of Denmark, younger daughter of Frederick II, to James VI in Oslo. Their second son became Charles I.

1590 John Napier, inventor and mathematician, of Balfron, who became the 8th Laird of Merchiston, invented the decimal point and started to develop natural logarithms. They were published in 1614 as the *Common Logarithm*.

1590. 'INVENTION' OF THE DECIMAL POINT.

1591 Dalry Mills produced the first paper manufactured in Scotland.

1592   James VI described Inverness as 'surrounded on all sides by the most aggressive and rebellious tribes, the clans'.

1593   The Border feud between the Johnstones and Maxwells, culminated with the Johnstones massacring a Maxwell contingent at Dryfe Sands, west of Lockerbie. The term 'Lockerbie lick' refers to the practice by the Johnstones of slashing the faces of defeated foes.

1594   The Battle of Glenlivet between forces under James VI and forces representing the 6th Earl of Huntly, who had links with Spain. Although Huntly's troops did well against an advance force, they fled when the main body arrived.

1595   Riot by Edinburgh High School pupils who had been refused a holiday. They took control of the school building and during the 'siege', a city bailie was killed.

1596   Dunderave Castle, near Inveraray, the *Castle Doom* of Neil Munro's novel, founded by Ian, Chief of the MacNaughtons.

1597   Parliament set the interest rate for money lending in Scotland at 10%; corporal punishment was to be meted out to anyone failing to comply.

1598   An Act was passed by Parliament, stating that all who claimed to own land in the Highlands and Islands, must produce their deeds before Scottish Privy Council.

1599 The first football match between teams representing Scotland and England, in Cumbria. Althought the score is not known, it resulted in a number of Englishmen being taken prisoner and one man was disembowelled (although he was apparently sewn up again!)

17TH CENTURY

1600   Sir John Carmichael, the Warden of the Middle Marches, was killed by a group of football hooligans, called Armstrong, on their way home from a match.

1601   At the General Assembly of the Church of Scotland at Burntisland, Fife, James VI put forth the concept of a new version of the bible. (Later, as James I of England, he promoted the Hampton Court Conference and the revised version bible).

1602   Following a raid on his property, Alexander Colquhoun of Luss was granted a Lieutenancy by James VI, to pursue the Clan Gregor. However, his troops were routed by the MacGregors the following year, at the battle of Glen Fruin.

1603   Union of Crowns of Scotland and England. James VI at the age of 37, became James I of England, through his great-grandmother having been Margaret Tudor.

1604   Allaster, the son of Gregor Roy, who had been outlawed for attacking the Colquhouns in Glen Fruin, was executed. The name of MacGregor was proscribed. (In 1633, it became legal to kill MacGregors and to hunt them with bloodhounds).

1605 The merchants and tradesmen of Glasgow organised themselves into a guild.

1606 John Welch, John Knox's son-in-law, was banished to France for his adherence to Presbyterianism. He was allowed to return to London in 1622.

1607 Forty seven revisers, the most eminent scholars and divines of the day, divided into groups dealing with various sections of the bible, and commenced work on the authorised verslon.

1608 Court held at Aros Castle, Isle of Mull, by James VI's Commissioner, to try numerous Highland chiefs.

1609 The principal Highland chiefs attended a conference in Iona where they pledged themselves to observe Bishop Andrew Knox's 'Statutes of Iona'. The Statutes sought to make the chiefs responsible for the good behaviour of their clansmen.

1610 Birth in Fife of James Wemyss, 'The Gunner'. He was appointed master gunner to Charles I in 1638, changed sides during the Civil War and then served as master gunner for Charles II. He patented an improved version of the leather gun.

1611 King James version of the bible produced. It superseded the Geneva Bible.

1612 Death from typhoid of Henry, Prince of Wales, eldest son of James VI and Queen Anne of Denmark. He had been heir to the throne of England and Scotland.

1613 King James VI made a handsome gift of books
to the library of St Andrews University;
then refused to pay for them.

1614 Donald MacKay, 1st Lord Reay, succeeded his
father, Hugh MacKay of Farr, as Head of the Clan
MacKay. He raised a regiment from amongst his
clansmen and took them to fight Christian IV of
Denmark, where they were called the 'Invincible
Regiment'.

1615 Birth of John Blackadder, the covenanting
minister of Troqueer, near Dumfries; he was
arrested in 1681 and died a prisoner on the Bass
Rock.

1616 Birth of Robert Edward, the minister and
musician, in Dundee. He graduated at St Andrews
in 1632 and ministered at Kirkmichael and
Murroes. His common place book of music contains
over 150 Scottish tunes and songs, and is deemed to
be the principal source of Scottish 16th- and 17th-
century music.

1617 James VI visited Dumfries and presented a silver
gun as a prize for marksmanship.

1618 The Five Articles of Perth were drawn up, by
which, at the General Assembly in Perth, James VI's
proposals on the Christian calendar and communion
were accepted.

1619 The Church of Cawdor, sometimes called
'Campbeltown', was built near the Castle of
Cawdor, Nairnshire.

1620 The village of Ceres in Fife was made a Burgh of Barony. The Ceres Games, held in June each year on the green, commemorate the return of the Ceres men from the Battle of Bannockburn.

1621 John Leslie became the 6th Earl of Rothes. He opposed Charles I's reintroduction of the Prayer Book and in 1638 helped draft the Covenant.

1622 Death of Andrew Melville in exile in France. He was Principal of Glasgow University and then Rector of St Andrews University. Known for his forthright views, he once told James VI that he was not king of the church but just 'God's silly vassal', for which he was banished to the Tower of London for five years.

1623 Samuel Rutherford, the future Covenanter, was appointed Professor of Latin at Edinburgh University. He became Rector of St Andrews University in 1639.

1624 An Order was passed by the City Fathers in Edinburgh that thatch was forbidden for use in house roofs, due to the risk of 'fire and falling'.

1625 Order from Charles I (who had assumed the throne this year from James VI) that doocots, houses built to keep pigeons for their meat and eggs, should not have stone floors, as the dung was a rich source of potassium nitrate, ie saltpetre, an ingredient of gunpowder. When mixed with the soil, it was more efficient.

1626 Thomas Hamilton, the Advocate, was appointed Lord Privy Seal. He was better known as 'Tam o' the Cowgate', so called by James VI because his mansion was in that district.

1627 Birth of David Gregory, the physician, in Drumoak, Aberdeenshire. He invented a military cannon superior to the technology of the day. It was destroyed at the request of Isaac Newton who was concerned at its potential. (Gregory also fathered 32 children.)

1628 Braemar Castle in Aberdeenshire was built by John Erskine, the 2nd Earl of Mar, as a replacement for the ruined Kindrochit Castle.

1629 Birth of Sir Ewan Dubh, 18th Chief of the Cameron Clan. He supported the Stewart kings and fought a guerrilla campaign against Cromwell's forces.

1630 Birth of Andrew Balfour, physician, at Demmiln, Fife. He realised the need for medicinal plants and founded the physic garden in Edinburgh, the forerunner of the Royal Botanic Garden.

1631 The start of the production of salt in Joppa, near Portobello, by evaporating seawater using coal from the local mines.

1632 Force of 2,000 men raised by Sir John Hepburn of Athelstaneford in East Lothian, for service in France. This Scottish brigade were known as 'Pontius Pilate's Bodyguards', and upon returning to Scotland, after the Restoration, they became the 'Royal Scots'.

1633 Charles I's first visit to Scotland. He was crowned Charles I at Holyrood by Archbishop Spottiswoode. His coronation banquet was held in the Great Hall of Edinburgh Castle.

1634 Hundreds perished in a famine in the North of Scotland and Orkney, which caused people to resort to eating dogs, seaweed and grass.

1635 Birth of Patrick Gordon, near Ellon in Aberdeenshire. He was a mercenary soldier who fought in the Swedish War against the Poles (1653-61), being repeatedly captured and fighting for his captors until he was recaptured by the other side. He became Governor of Kiev and a personal friend of Tsar Peter the Great.

1636 The new tolbooth was erected in Glasgow at the corner of High Street and Trongate. It replaced the original tolbooth at Glasgow Cross.

1637 Riot in St Giles Cathedral, Edinburgh, over the introduction of the Scottish prayer book (*Book of Common Prayer*). A Tron kail-wife, Jenny Geddes, flung her stool at the Dean shouting 'Deil colic the wame o' ye!' (May the devil buckle your belly).

1638 The National Covenant drawn up and signed in Greyfriars' Kirk, Edinburgh. It abolished Episcopacy.

1639 The Covenanters took control of the country. King Charles was forced to accept the 'Pacification of Berwick'.

1640 The Ogilvy stronghold of Forter Castle in Glen Isla, Angus, was sacked by the Earl of Argyll's Covenanters.

1641 Scotland's first newspaper, *The Diurnal Occurences Touching the Dailie Procedings in Parliament*, was printed in Edinburgh.

1642 James, the 1st Duke of Hamilton, tried to dissuade the Covenanter leaders from supporting the English Parliamentarians in the Civil War.

1643 The Solemn League and Covenant was drawn up. Primarily it was to have the Church of England adopt a Scottish pattern, in return for the Scottish army assisting the Parliamentarians in England.

1644 The Battle of Tippiemuir when the Royalists under James Graham, 1st Marquis of Montrose, defeated the Covenanters, led by Lord Elcho, near the village of Tippiemuir, four miles from Perth.

1645 Montrose's campaign on behalf of Charles I. He was defeated at Philiphaugh, Selkirk. However he had a resounding victory at the Battle of Alford, in Aberdeenshire, over Covenanting forces.

1646 The great plague of Glasgow – thousands were left sick and dying.

1647 The Tron Kirk in the High Street, Edinburgh, was opened for worship, though the building, started in 1637 was not completed until 1663. It was designed to house the congregation displaced from St Giles when it became an Episcopal Cathedral.

1648 Birth of Richard Cameron, the Covenanter leader, in Falkland, Fife. Following exile in Holland he put together an army of extremists called the 'Cameronians'. (See 1680).

1649 The Scots proclaimed Charles II king after the execution of Charles I. (Charles I was the last king to be born in Scotland, at Dumfermline in 1600. Charles II was the last king to be crowned in Scotland, at Scone in 1651).

1650 Epidemic of the 'Irish Ague' in Scotland, ie a very sore pain in the head. Treatment was by tying up the head tightly in bandages.

* Trans:
`I've just invented
a new international
language -'

1651 The first artificial international language, 'inter-language' was devised and published by Aberdonian, George Dalgarno.

1652 The Great Fire of Glasgow consumed a third of the City. As a result Glasgow's candle factories were removed from the old City Centre, to the Cornriggs on the west of the City.

1653 The start of the Cromwell regime. Many castles were stormed in Scotland by the Roundheads, including Blair Castle at Blair Atholl.

1654 Marian, the daughter of George Foulis, the goldsmith of Colinton, Edinburgh, was abducted by a musician, Andrew Hill. The judge delayed sentence on Hill for 15 days during which time Hill was eaten by vermin in prison.

1655 The Burgesses of Glasgow's right to elect their own magistrates, removed in 1652, was restored by Oliver Cromwell.

1656 Birth of 'Blind Harper', the Gaelic poet and harpist, (Rory Dall Morrison of Braga, Lewis). He is remembered particularly for the lament, *Wednesday's Bereavement*.

1657 First use of the term Whigs (to spur on) for dissenting Presbyterians or Covenanters. (After 1687 it applied to anyone supporting the 'Williamite' Revolution and after that a label for people who opposed Jacobites and Tories).

1658 A great storm caused havoc in Dundee, with the harbour area being completely destroyed.

1659 The Merchants' House was built at the Bridgegate, Glasgow, for commercial and social activities.

1660 Charles II was restored to the throne of Scotland. On being told of the restoration, Sir Thomas Urquhart, the writer, died of an uncontrollable fit of laughter.

1661 Birth of Patrick Blair, a doctor, who gained renown for being the first person to scientifically dissect an elephant. The elephant, part of a travelling fair, had died on the road between Broughty Ferry and Dundee.

1662 Birth of James Douglas, the 2nd Duke of Queensberry, 'The Union Duke'. He attended Glasgow University and served under John Graham of Claverhouse ('Bonnie Dundee'). It is said he coped with the traumas of the Darien collapse by taking to his bed for the whole of 1700.

1661   Birth of Blair
first dissector of an elephant.

1663   John Hay, the 2nd Earl and 1st Marquis of
Tweeddale, was appointed President of the Privy
Council. He was later made the scapegoat for the
Darien Scheme. (See 1698).

1664   The Linningshaugh area, at the foot of the
Saltmarket, was purchased and added to Glasgow
Green, which then stretched from Stockwell Street
to St Enoch's Burn.

1665   Birth of songwriter, Lady Grizel Baillie, of
Polwarth, who wrote *Were'na My Heart Licht, I
Wad Die*.

1666   The 'Pentland Rising' which started in Dalry,
Kirkcudbrightshire, when Covenanters went to the
rescue of an old farmer, threatened with torture by

dragoons, for failing to pay government fees. It ended with the Rout of the Covenanters at Rullion Green by the Pentland Hills.

1667 The birth of John Arbuthnot, physician and literary humorist, in Kincardineshire. He was physician to Queen Anne and became well known on the literary scene in London. He wrote, amongst others, *The Act of Political Lying*.

1668 A Covenanter sniper in Edinburgh shot at, (but missed) James Sharp, Archbishop of St Andrews. The Archbishop was murdered in 1679 while crossing Magus Moor, near St Andrews.

1669 The first 'Declaration of Indulgence' to conciliate moderate resistance of the Covenanters. It resulted in 43 deprived ministers being restored to their parishes.

1670 Birth of Billy Marshall in Kirkudbright. He was a tinker who gained a formidable reputation as a boxer, bandit, smuggler and an army and navy deserter. He had illegitimate children beyond number, and four were fathered after he acheived the age of 100. He took whisky to excess and died at an age of over 120 years.

1671 Golf match between John Paterson, a leather golf ball manufacturer, partnered by the Duke of York (later James VII) against two Englishmen of the Court of Holyrood Palace. It was played over Leith Links and Paterson and the Duke won. With his winnings Paterson built the tenement building, 'Golfer's Land'.

1672   A Decree was issued that all who use arms in
Scotland, should submit them to the Lord Lyon,
King of Arms.

1673   Birth of George Wade. the soldier and road builder.
Although Irish, he is remembered for the period
1724-40 when he was Commander in Chief, North
Britain, during which time he built 240 miles of
military roads in the Highlands. He is the only
commoner mentioned in the National Anthem. (See
1724)

1674   The first cargo of Virginia tobacco arrived in Glasgow.

1675   Death of Sir William Lockhart of Lee, the soldier
and diplomat. He fought at the Battles of Preston
and Worcester; he married Oliver Cromwell's neice.

1676   The founding of the Royal Company of Archers,
the Queen's bodyguard in Scotland. They still
attend Her Majesty on official occasions in
Scotland. Officers bear swords, and archers both
swords and long bows.

1677 Fines passed by Edinburgh Council on citizens whose houses were not built of stone and covered with slates or tiles.

1678 Publication of MacKenzie's *Laws and Customs of Scotland in Matters Criminal*, which form the basis of a number of Scottish principles in criminal cases.

1679 Following the 'Declaration of Rutherglen' against the victory by Covenanters over the forces of John Graham of Claverhouse at Drumclog, the covenanting forces were defeated at Bothwell Brig.

1680 Battle of Airds Moss near Cumnock, Ayrshire. Dragoons sent by General Tam Dalyell brought a crushing defeat on the Covenanters; among those killed was Richard Cameron. (See 1648)

1681 The first piped water supply (wooden pipes) was led to Castlehill, Edinburgh, from Comiston Springs.

1682 Birth of William Aikman, near Arbroath. He was a portrait painter of renown, painting the royals, the Prime Minister Sir Robert Walpole and the Duke of Argyll.

1683 A Scottish beaver hat factory was inaugurated in Edinburgh by the merchant, Thom Hamilton, who imported beaver and racoon skins from North America.

1684 Birth of Allan Ramsay, the poet, in Leadhills. After a time as a bookseller in Edinburgh, he became a theatrical impresario, then a poet and collector of ballads. His most famous work is *The Gentle Shepherd*, much praised by Burns.

1685 Death of the 'Wigtown Martyrs'. Two women, Margaret MacLachlan and Margaret Wilson, were found guilty of being Conventiclers. They were tied to stakes at the mouth of the River Bladnoch in Wigtown Bay and drowned by the incoming tide.

1686 The building of the Leighton Library in Dunblane, Perthshire. It was built to house the Bishop of Dunblane's book collection and is deemed to be the oldest purpose-built library in Scotland.

1687 Death of Sir John Nesbet, Lord Dirleton, renowned for his pursuit of Covenanters and the publication of *Doubts and Questions in the Law of Scotland*, known as 'Dirleton's Doubts'.

1688 Birth of James Francis Edward Stewart, 'The Old Pretender', in St James' Palace, London. Brought up in France, he was assured of support in

Scotland for the Stewart cause when he landed.
Through ill weather and the arrival of the English
fleet, an attempt in 1708 was aborted. A further
expedition (see 1715) also proved unsuccessful. He
married the 15-year-old daughter of the King of
Poland in 1719 and died in Rome in 1766.

1689 Battle of the Pass of Killiecrankie, near
Pitlochry. John Graham of Claverhouse was killed,
though his troops won the day against the Williamite
troops under Sir Thomas Livingston.

1690 At the Battle of Cromdale, east of Grantown
in Moray, the Jacobites lost over 300 men to
Williamite troops under Sir Thomas Livingston.

1691 The Treaty of Achallander when the Jacobite
leaders were summoned by John Campbell, Earl of
Achallander, to agree an armistice in their fight to
restore James VII to the British throne.

1692 Massacre of Glencoe on 6th February. Two
companies of the Earl of Argyle's Regiment who
were quartered with the MacDonalds in Glencoe,
acting on Government orders, killed 38 of the clan.

1693 The Scottish Parliament, keen to promote the
making of linen in Scotland, passed a ruling that all
corpses had to be buried in plain linen and relatives
of the deceased must swear an oath to this effect.

1694 The Bank of England was established primarily
by Sir William Paterson of Tinwald, Dumfriesshire.
(He supported the Darien Scheme and sailed with
the ill-fated expedition in 1698.)

1695   The Company of the Bank of Scotland was founded as a public bank by an Act of the Parliament of Scotland. The position of Governor was created at the same time.

1696   The execution, for heresy, of Edinburgh student, Thomas Aikenhead.

1697   Greenlaw became the county town of Berwickshire. The decision was made by Sir Patrick Hume of Polwarth, Lord Chancellor of Scotland. (In 1903 Greenlaw's county town status passed to Duns).

1698   The ill-fated Darien venture, when a Scottish expedition of five ships, filled with settlers and traders, set off for the Darien coast on the isthmus of Panama. The objective of finding an overseas outlet for Scottish products failed through the intervention of the Spanish, fever and feuds, in this ill-conceived scheme.

1699   Hailes Castle, East Linton in East Lothian, which had been badly damaged by Cromwell's troops in 1650, was sold by the Seton family to David Dalrymple, later Lord Hailes.

18TH CENTURY

1700 The hanging of the fiddler and freebooter, James MacPherson, in Banff. He offered his fiddle to the crowd but as there were no takers, he snapped it in two. Remembered by Robert Burns in *MacPherson's Farewell*.

1701 Cockfighting, for which Edinburgh was famous throughout Britain, was banned by the City Council.

COCK FIGHTING

1702 Accession of Anne Stewart, daughter of James VII, to the thrones of Scotland and England.

1703 William Carstares, 'Cardinal Carstares', from Cathcart, Glasgow, became Principal of Edinburgh University. He had previously been implicated in plots against Charles II and was imprisoned and tortured. He was also one of the founders of the Episcopal Church of Scotland.

1704 The Act of Security was the Scottish response to the English 1701 Act of Settlement. The act reserved the right for the Scottish Parliament to nominate its own successor to the crown, unless the sovereignty of Scotland had first been guaranteed.

1705 The Alien Act was passed by the English Parliament. It was an ultimatum that if the Scots did not accept Hanoverian succession, or if negotiations for union did not get under way, the Scots would be deemed 'aliens' and there would be an embargo on Scottish goods.

1706 Proposals for union with England caused patriotic mobs to gather in Edinburgh and Glasgow.

1707 Act of Union between Scottish and English Parliaments. It was ratified by the Scottish Parliament, which then dissolved. (Later referred to by Robert Burns as a 'parcel of rogues, selling independence for English gold'). (See 2000).

1708 Death of John Hamilton, the 2nd Lord Belhaven, the well remembered anti-unionist who made his famous speech in 1706 which is much quoted by Scottish Nationalists.

1709 Birth of Dr Samuel Johnson in Lichfield. Initially a parliamentary journalist , he produced a dictionary in 1755 which brought great acclaim. Toured the Highlands in the company of James Boswell and through his opinionated, cantankerous views achieved lasting fame. (See 1773).

1710 Birth of Helen Walker, a farmer's daughter from Dalwhairn in Kirkcudbrightshire. She refused to commit perjury at her sister's trial but walked to London barefoot to successfully obtain a reprieve for her. She became 'Jeanie Deans', the heroine of Scott's, *The Heart of Midlothian*.

1711 John Scott formed his shipyard company in Greenock to build fishing and small coastal craft.

1712 The Patronage Act passed which reimposed civil interference in ecclesiastical appointments.

1713 A Bill before the Westminster Parliament to repeal the Act of Union lost by only four votes.

1714 Queen Anne died and was succeeded by her cousin, George Lewis of Hanover.

1715 The first Jacobite rising when John, 6th Earl of Mar (called 'Bobbing John' as he continually changed sides) raised the standard of James Francis Edward Stewart, the Old Pretender. It culminated in the Battle of Sheriffmuir, north-east of Dunblane, when the Highlanders and the King's men both claimed victory.

There's some say that we wan, some say that
*   they wan,*
Some say that nane wan at a', man
But one thing I'm sure, that at Sheriffmuir,
A battle there was which I saw, man,
And we ran, and they ran, and they ran,
*   and we ran,*
And we ran, and they ran awa', man!

1716 The Disarming Act was passed by the Government, imposing fines for possessing arms and requesting their surrender. The Jacobites imported broken and useless arms from Holland and handed those over.

1717 The 'Auchterarder Creed' was issued by the local presbytery, stating that God's chosen elect need not foresake sin!

1718 Death of physician Robert Erskine from Alva, who went to Russia and became doctor to Peter the Great. Erskine was in overall charge of Russia's medical services and encouraged many Scottish doctors and scientists to make their career in the service of the Tsar.

1719 Belhaven Brewery, Scotland's oldest surviving brewery, was established.

1720 Birth of Prince Charles Edward Stewart, 'The Young Pretender', in Rome. He was the son of the 'Old Pretender', James Francis Edward and Clementina, the grand-daughter of the King of Poland. Died in Rome in 1788 (see 1722, 1740, 1745, 1746).

1721 Death of Alexander Selkirk of Largo, Fife, who in 1704 lived on the uninhabited South Pacific island of Juan Fernandez, 800 miles off the coast of Chile. He was marooned for four years and four months and was the inspiration for Daniel Defoe's novel of 1719, *Robinson Crusoe*.

It happened one day, about noon, going towards my boat, I was exceedingly surprised with the print of a man's naked foot on the shore.

1722 Birth of Flora MacDonald in South Uist. In 1746 she helped smuggle Prince Charles Edward Stewart (dressed as 'Betty Burke', an Irish maidservant) from Benbecula to Portree.

1723 Birth of Adam Smith, the economist and philosopher, in Kirkaldy. Studied at Glasgow University then lectured at Balliol College, Oxford, before being appointed Professor of Logic at Glasgow in 1751. His *Wealth of Nations* contains fundamental philosophical principles on the science of economics.

1724 Lord Lovat sent a letter to George I warning him of unrest in the Highlands. Major-General George Wade was dispatched to reconnoitre. He reported that there were 12,000 men, 'ready to rise in favour of the Pretender'. (see 1673).

1725 The English Malt Tax was extended to Scotland thereby increasing the price of ale by threepence per barrel. It resulted in the Shawfield Riots when the mob took to the streets and sacked Shawfield House, Glassford Street, Glasgow, the home of the

local MP, Daniel Campbell, who had voted in favour
of the tax. With his compensation he purchased the
island of Islay.

1726   Birth of William Roy in Miltonhead. He is
       remembered as a surveyor who in 1784 started the
       first trigonometrical survey of Britain.

1727   The Royal Bank of Scotland was founded in
       Edinburgh. It was supported by John Campbell,
       2nd Duke of Argyll and had mostly Whig
       supporters.

1728   Maggie Dickson ('Half Hangit Maggie') a fishwife,
       was hanged in Edinburgh's Grassmarket. As her
       coffin was being taken for burial in Musselburgh,
       noises were heard from within. Revived by a stiff
       dram she was allowed to go free, subsequently
       giving birth to a number of children and ultimately
       dying of old age.

1729   The main General Wade road was built in the
       Highlands; from Dunkeld to Inverness.

1730 Birth of Peter Wilson of Aboyne, who in 1738 was playing on the quay at Aberdeen when he was kidnapped, taken to America and sold in Philadelphia for $30 to a man originally from Perth. He married the daughter of a planter, was attacked and captured by Indians, escaped and caught by the French who then shipped him from Quebec to England. He eventually published his memoirs and opened a tavern in Edinburgh.

1731 The military road, across the Corrieyairack Pass, from Laggan to Fort Augustus, was completed by George Wade.

1732 The birth of John Broadwood in Cockburnspath, near Edinburgh; he designed and made the world's first grand piano.

1733 Death of JP, Sir Robert Grierson of Lag, responsible for the prosecution of Conventiclers, and who had presided over the trial and execution of the Wigtown Martyrs. He was known to the Covenanters as 'the worst villain Scotland ever gave birth to'.

1734 Death of Rob Roy MacGregor, the legendary outlaw. In 1712 a warrant was issued for his arrest when MacGregor's chief drover absconded with a loan of £1,000 from the Duke of Montrose. He twice escaped from imprisonment and was pardoned in Inverkeithing, by General Wade in 1725.

1735 The birth of Samuel Greig, Admiral of the Russian Navy. Following a recruitment drive by Catherine the Great for British officers to join the Russian Navy, Greig joined in 1764, becoming a full Admiral

in 1782. In 1788 he commanded the Russian naval
fleet in the war against Sweden. He died the same
year and received a state funeral in Russia.

1736 The chief of the Clan Gunn was charged at
Sutherland Regality Court at Dornoch with claiming
payment on a forged bill. He asked to see the actual
bill and then fought off the whole court with a chair
while he swallowed it!

1737 The 'winnowing machine' was invented by Andrew
Roper of Hawick.

1738 Birth of Elizabeth Buchan, in Irvine, who founded
the Buchanites. She claimed to see visions of the
day when all her followers would be taken up to
heaven.

1739 The first edition of *The Scots Magazine*, the world's
oldest periodical.

1740 Hugh and Robert Tennent started their brewing
company in Edinburgh.

1741 Dredging commenced on the River Clyde, as no
ships of any real draught could go beyond
Dumbarton.

1742 Religious revivals took place in Cambuslang
and Kilsyth. Called the 'Awakening', they were led
by Rev William McCulloch and Rev John Roble,
assisted by Wesley's associate, George Whitfield.

1743 Birth, in Edinburgh, of Gilbert Stuart, the historian.
In his major work, *'View of Society in Europe*, he
challenged the views of the 'Scottish enlightenment'.

1744 The oldest golf club in the world, The Honourable Company of Edinburgh Golfers, played its first competition for a silver cup on the Links of Leith . (St Andrews Golf Club was established 10 years later.)

1745 Second Jacobite Rising. Bonnie Prince Charlie landed at Moidart, raised his standard and put together a force. He then took Perth, and at Prestonpans, near Edinburgh, defeated government forces.

1746 The last battle on British soil, at Culloden on Drummossie Muir, near Inverness, was fought between the Jacobites, under Prince Charles Edward Stewart and the Hanoverians led by the Duke of Cumberland. The ill-prepared clansmen were routed and no quarter was taken.

1747 'Act of Proscription' introduced in the aftermath of Culloden. The Act banned the wearing of tartan and Highland dress by any but the military. Offenders were given six months in jail for a first offence, transportation to the penal colonies for a second.

1748 At the tolbooth in Stonehaven, three ministers locked in a cell baptised babies by pouring water on to them through the window bars.

1749 The first Edinburgh to London stagecoach, called the 'Glass Machine', left the Whitehorse Inn, off the Canongate, Edinburgh. It took 14 days to complete the journey.

1750 The highest village in the Highlands, Tomintoul in Banffshire, was founded by the 4th Duke of Gordon. (The nearby Lecht to Cockbridge road is invariably the first road in Scotland closed by snow each year.)

1751 The Cramond Iron Works was established at Cockle Mill by the Smith and Wrightwork Company of Leith. They manufactured the first commercially produced Scottish crude steel.

1752 The assassination of the 'Red Fox', Colin Campbell of Glenure, in the wood of Lettermore, Appin, Argyll. James Stewart, 'James of the Glens', was later hanged at Ballachulish for a murder he denied committing. The murder is central to the plot of Robert Louis Stevenson's *Kidnapped* and was the beginning of the end of the clan system in the Highlands.

1753 Archibald Cameron, brother of the chief of the Camerons, who had been a doctor and ADC to Prince Charles Edward Stewart, was executed in Edinburgh; the last person to die for the Jacobite cause.

1754 The Society of St Andrews Golfers was established. St Andrews is now recognised internationally as the home of golf. (Golf has been played on the links there since the 12th century).

1755 Birth of Sir Alexander MacKenzie in Inverness. In 1789, while employed by the Hudson's Bay Company, he set off with eight native Indians in two canoes across the Great Slave Lake and along a vast

river, which is now called after him. He became the
first white man to travel coast-to-coast across North
America.

1756 The birth of John Loudon McAdam in Ayr. He
amassed a fortune during the American Revolution
and back in Britain he acquired control of the
British Tar Company and introduced hard-wearing
road surfaces. The term 'tarmacadamed' described
the use of graduated stones set in bitumen. He is
buried in Moffat.

1757 The birth of Sir David Baird, soldier, at Newbyth,
East Lothian. He was held prisoner in India for 44
months, chained to a fellow prisoner. Baird's
mother is on record as pitying the man chained to
'Our Davie'. He fought campaigns in Egypt, Africa
and Denmark and on four occasions Parliament
passed a vote of thanks to him after splendid
victories.

1758 The birth, in Edinburgh, of Alexander Nasmyth,
the painter and achitect. He became one of the
most influential landscape painters in the history of
Scottish painting.

1759 Birth of Robert Burns, Scotland's national bard.
Burns Suppers are celebrated worldwide on or near
the date of his birth, 25th January. His *Auld Lang
Syne* (1788) has been universally adopted as the
song of parting.

1760 The foundation of Carron Iron Works at
Falkirk, for the smelting of ironstone.

1761 The birth of the eminent soldier, Sir John Moore, in Glasgow. He saw service during the American War of Independence, in Corsica, the West Indies, Ireland, Holland and Egypt. He was in charge of the entire British Army in 1808 in the conflict with Napoleon. He is remembered for a famous 250-mile march to Corunna, Spain, in midwinter, where he was killed.

1762 George Younger started a company brewing ale in Alloa.

1763 St Cecilia's Concert Hall was built in the Cowgate, Edinburgh, by Robert Mylne, for the Edinburgh Musical Society. The acoustics were deemed to be perfect for the conveyance of sound.

1764 Death of Annie Laurie, the subject of the song. Annie was born in Maxwelton House near Moniaive. The early version of the song is thought to have been written by William Douglas, a Jacobite Officer. Although he wrote 'For Annie Laurie I'd lay me doon and dee', he married a Miss Clerk of Glenboig. Annie married an Alexander Ferguson.

1765 The level of Carlingwark Loch, in Kirkcud-brightshire, was lowered to allow easier access to the massive deposits of marle, (clay used as manure).

1766 The birth of Thomas Bruce, 7th Earl of Elgin and 11th Earl of Kincardine. He was a soldier, diplomat and art connoisseur and was responsible for the Parthenon Frieze and other ancient trophies being shipped out of Athens; they are now known as the 'Elgin Marbles' and are housed in the British Museum.

1767 An expedition to the 'Southern Continent', where the midshipman of the scoop *Swallow*, Robert Pitcairn from Glasgow, was the first to spot the island which now bears his name. It later became famous as the home of the bounty mutineers.

1768 Glasgow's Broomielaw Bridge was opened.

1769 James Watt of Greenock's steam engine was patented as a 'separate condenser'. Watt also produced the original formula to define horsepower.

1770 James Bruce, the explorer from Stirling, who was nicknamed 'The Abyssinian', became the first white man to see the source of the Blue Nile.

1771 The first *Encyclopaedia Britannica* in three volumes was published by Bell and MacFarquhar of Edinburgh; William Smellie was the Editor.

1772 The marriage, by proxy, of Prince Charles Edward Stewart and Louise Maximiliana Emmanuela (the Countess of Albany).

1773 James Boswell, the Publisher and Biographer, together with Dr. Samuel Johnson, undertook an extensive tour of Scotland and the Hebrides. Boswell's famous *Journal of a Tour to the Hebrides* was published in 1785. (See 1709).

1774 John Paul Jones from Kirkbean, Kirkcudbrightshire, settled in Virginia. The following year he commanded the first naval vessel procured by Congress, the *Alfred*, and subsequently founded the American Navy.

1771 First Encyclopaedia
      Britannica .

1775 New Port Glasgow and Newark, 20 miles down
the Clyde from Glasgow, were formed into the new
port for Glasgow, Port Glasgow.

1776 Death in Edinburgh of the great philosopher
and diplomat, David Hume. His essays on morality,
politics and human nature significantly influenced
the lives and works of many, including Adam Smith
and his *Wealth of Nations*.

1777 Glasgow's first street pavement was built in
Candleriggs, from Trongate to Bell Street. As a
result, Glasgow Town Council employed a third man
to clean the streets of the City!

1778 Burial of the great Gaelic bard Rob Donn MacKay,
at Balnakil in Sutherland. (His poems were not
published until 1829).

1779 The first census of the island of Iona was carried out by the estate of the 5th Duke of Argyll. The inhabitants totalled 249.

1780 George Square, Glasgow, was laid out in the lands of Deanston, as an expansive residential development on the then western fringe of the city. It was named in honour of George III.

1781 The founding of the Society of the Antiquaries of Scotland by David Stewart Erskine, the 11th Earl of Buchan, for the preservation of Scotland's antiquities.

1782 Repeal of the Act of Proscription which prohibited the use of Highland dress (see 1747).

1783 Scotland's National Academy of Science, the Royal Society of Edinburgh (RSE) was formed. Sir Walter Scott was its President from 1820 to 1832.

1784 The first manned balloon ascent in Britain by Scotsman, James 'Balloon' Tytler, reaching a height of 350 ft (107m) over Edinburgh's Abbeyhill district. (He was also editor of the second edition of the *Encyclopedia Britannica*).

1785 The start of the Clearances when tens of thousands of clansfolk were removed from their homes and crofts to make way for the large scale farming of sheep in the Highlands and Islands.

1786 First edition of Robert Burns works, printed in Kilmarnock by John Wilson.

1787 Strike by the Calton Weavers of Glasgow. The Riot
Act was read to a crowd of over 7,000 and the
military opened fire, with the result that six strikers
were killed. (See 1820).

1788 The execution of Deacon William Brodie in
Edinburgh. He was a town councillor by day and
the leader of a gang of thieves at night. He is said to
have inspired Robert Louis Stevenson's *The
Strange Case of Dr Jekyll and Mr Hyde.*

1789 The birth of William Collins, the publisher, in
Eastwood, Renfrewshire. He started the business in
1819 in conjunction with Charles Chalmers,
printing school textbooks and temperance tracts.
(He was a member of the Temperance Movement).

1790 The Forth and Clyde canal running between
Bowling near Dumbarton and Grangemouth was
opened. It had taken 22 years to complete.

1791 The start of the 23-year period when 'Blacksmith' Joseph Paisley conducted weddings at Gretna in Dumfriesshire.

1792 Birth of Arthur Anderson in Shetland. He helped found the P&O shipping line; also founded Shetland's first newspaper in 1836 and the Anderson High School in 1862.

1793 Sir Walter Scott met Robert Paterson who was cleaning the famous Covenanter's Stone (commemorating nine Covenanters who died at Dunnottar Castle) at Dunnottar Parish Church in Stonehaven. This meeting provided the inspiration for Scott's novel, *Old Mortality*.

1794 The 100th Regiment (Gordon Highlanders), was raised by the Duke of Gordon. All recruits were promised a kiss from the Duchess of Gordon's lips.

1794 Gordon Highlander recruits
promised a kiss from the Duchess

1795 The painting of 'The Penny Wedding' (National Galleries of Scotland) a portrayal of Scottish customs by the Scottish painter, David Allan, from Alloa.

1796 Death of James Wilson, a native of St Andrews and a graduate of its university, who emigrated to the American Colonies in 1765. He became one of the first Justices of the Supreme Court and in 1776 one of the signatories of the Declaration of Independence.

1797 John Pinkerton, the Edinburgh lawyer and historian, published his now famous *History of Scotland from the Accession of the House of Stewart to Mary*.

1798 Application by David Wilkie, the painter, to enter the Trustees' Academy in Edinburgh, which he did the following year. One of the best known Scottish painters, his exhibition at the Victoria and Albert Museum in 1822 required crush barriers to hold back the crowds.

1799 Death of Lieutenant Alexander Smollett of Bonhill at the Battle of Alkmaar, Holland. Alexandria, in Dumbartonshire, is called after him.

19TH CENTURY

1800 The birth in Peebles of William Chambers, the Edinburgh publisher. The *Chambers Encyclopedia* was published between 1859 and 1868 in 520 weekly parts. He was elected Lord Provost of Edinburgh and ordered the massive restoration of St Giles at his own expense.

1801 The Crinan Canal was opened between Ardrishaig and Crinan to save shipping from the Clyde and Loch Fyne having to go around the Mull of Kintyre. It is some nine miles long and was designed by John Rennie of Phantassie, East Lothian.

1802 The world's first steam tug, the 58ft-long *Charlotte Dundas*, towed two laden barges along the Forth and Clyde Canal.

1803 Thomas Douglas, 5th Earl of Selkirk, as a result of the Clearances, led over 800 emigrants to found a settlement on Prince Edward Island.

1804 The clerk of the Duddingston Curling Society in Edinburgh inserted the club's rules into the minutes book; as a result they became the established worldwide Rules of Curling.

1805 Birth at Todrigg Farm, near Kilmarnock, of Johnnie Walker, who was to establish a grocery and spirit shop in the town and eventually produce the blend of whisky bearing his name which is world-famous.

1806 Death of Mungo Park, the explorer, by drowning in Nigeria. Born in 1771 in Foulshiels in the Yarrow valley, he first journeyed to the Gambia into unmapped territory with only six African companions and did not reappear for another 18 months. Although he later became a doctor in Selkirk, he set off again in 1804 for his final, ill-fated journey.

1807 A ship coming up the Clyde fired her guns in salute at the Tail of the Bank, off Greenock. The shot went through the roof of Laird's Ropeworks, then struck a tenement flat narrowly missing the lady inside.

1808 The birth in Edinburgh of James Nasmyth, the inventor of the steam hammer, the steam pile driver and the creator of the concept of manufacturing assembly lines.

1809 Long-distance walk by Captain Robert Barclay of Udny, of 1,000 miles in 1,000 hours to win a bet of 1,000 guineas. On a specially prepared course near Newmarket he successfully covered one mile in every consecutive hour over 42 days, lost 32 lbs, and won his wager.

1810 The first savings bank was instituted at Ruthwell in Dumfriesshire, by the Rev Henry Duncan of Lochrutton in Kirkcudbrightshire. An energetic man, he had also established the *Dumfries and Galloway Courier* in 1809.

1811 The first golfing championship for women. It was organised and competed in by the fishwives of Musselburgh.

1812 The launch of the *Comet*, the first steamship to ply commercially to and from Europe. She was built by John Wood & Co. of Port Glasgow for Henry Bell. Wrecked in 1820, her engine was salvaged and then utilised in a local sugar mill for many years.

1813 Birth of David Livingstone, the explorer and missionary, in Blantyre. He initially worked at a loom in the local cotton mill, then studied medicine at Glasgow University before training at the London Missionary Society. He converted over 30,000 people to Christianity during his three explorations in Africa and his efforts helped to end the slave trade. During his final expedition, to find the source of the Nile, he went 'missing' for many months and was found by the American journalist, Henry Morton Stanley, who greeted him with the immortal words, 'Doctor Livingstone, I presume?'

1814 The birth of Andrew Barclay of Kilbirnie, Ayrshire, who pioneered the 'fireless steam locomotive' which could operate in places where fire was a danger.

1815 Shoe manufacturing was established in Kilmarnock by the Clark family.

1816 St Andrews Cathedral, Aberdeen, was built by Archibald Simpson, in the Gothic Perpendicular style.

1817 First publication of *Blackwood's* monthly magazine in Edinburgh, by William Blackwood, bookseller and publisher. (It ceased publication in 1980).

1818 The inauguration of passenger steamboat services from Ireland to the Broomielaw in Glasgow.

1819 Birth of Alexander Melville Bell, father of Alexander Graham Bell, in Edinburgh. Like his son he was interested in teaching the deaf and developed a physiological alphabet called the Visible Speech System.

1820 The 'Battle of Bonnymuir' was brought about by unemployment, industrial unrest and demonstrations by weavers in Paisley and Glasgow in 1819. The 'battle' occured when some Calton weavers marched on Falkirk and were met by troops at Bonnymuir. Four people were wounded, 47 arrested of whom three were executed. (See 1787)

1821 Death of James Gregory from Aberdeen, the Professor of Medicine at Edinburgh University. He is remembered for devising the laxative, 'Gregory's mixture'.

1822 The Caledonian Canal opened. It connects Corpach, near Fort William, and Clachnaharry, near Inverness, a distance of some 60 miles and joins up various lochs. It was built to allow ships to avoid French privateers during the Napoleonic Wars as well as the rigours of the Pentland Firth.

1823 Start of jute spinning in Dundee, which ultimately resulted in over 50 factories processing 143,000 tons of imported jute each year by 1873.

1824 Birth of George MacDonald, the novelist and poet, in Huntly, Aberdeenshire. He graduated from Kings College, Aberdeen and after some time as a congregational minister resigned to dedicate himself to writing. His reputation today rests on his works of fantasy which influenced writers such as C S Lewis:

'Where did you come from, baby dear?'
'Out of the everywhere into here.'

1825 Birth of the tallest Scotsman and the tallest recorded
'true' (non-pathological) giant, as recorded in the
Guinness Book of Records. He was Angus MacAskill
of Berneray Island in the Sound of Harris. He stood
7ft 9in tall (2.36m) and could lift a hundredweight
(50kg) with two fingers and hold it at arm's length for
ten minutes. He died in Canada in 1863.

Birth of the Giant MacAskill

1826 The Scottish Banks were deemed exempt from the
British note issuing system and could continue to
issue one pound notes. This exemption was
championed by Sir Walter Scott. (Bank of Scotland
notes still carry his portrait.)

1827 Birth of William Fleming Vallance the famous
painter of sea and shipping scenes.

1828 James B Neilson invented the blast furnace. He
discovered that by raising the temperature of the
blast of air through the furnace, the amount of fuel
used in the smelting process was reduced.

1829 The hanging of William Burke, gravedigger and murderer, in Edinburgh. (His accomplice, William Hare, turned King's evidence.)

1830 James Loch of Edinburgh, the main instigator behind the notorious Sutherland Clearances, was appointed as MP for Wick and the Northern Burghs.

1831 The first reaping machine was invented by the Rev Patrick Bell of Carmylie, Renfrewshire.

1832 Death of Sir Walter Scott, the novelist and poet, who made a massive contribution to Scottish literature. Despite his own poliomyelitis and ill health his productivity rate in turning out works was phenomenal. Among his many poems, The *Lady of the Lake*, *Marmion* and *The Lay of the Last Minstrel* are world-famous. His novels include *Waverley*, *The Heart of Midlothian* and *Quentin Durward*.

O what a tangled web we weave, when first we practise to deceive!   *Marmion*, 1808

1833 The Murder of Rizzio (National Gallery of Scotland) was painted by Sir William Allan, the historical artist. (See 1566).

1834 The Society of St Andrews Golfers (established 1754) changed its name to the Royal and Ancient under the patronage of William IV (William III of Scotland).

1835 Death of James Hogg, 'the Ettrick Shepherd', who was a poet and novelist. His work in 1813, *The Queen's Wake*, about a poetry contest at the court of Queen Mary, made him famous. His *Private Memoirs and Confessions of a Justified Sinner* published in 1824 is deemed to be his masterpiece.

1836 Sir Charles Bell was appointed Professor of Surgery at Edinburgh. He had previously achieved fame through his research into the nervous system especially the facial and respiratory nerves. Paralysis of the seventh facial nerve is called Bell's Palsy.

1837 Birth of Dr Joseph Bell in Edinburgh. A surgeon, he was known for his remarkable powers of observation and deduction. In 1878 Arthur Conan Doyle enrolled in his clinical surgery class and stated later that Bell was the inspiration for his creation, Sherlock Holmes.

1838 Death of Anne Grant of Laggan, the poet and essayist. Born in Glasgow in 1755 she did not start writing until after the death of her husband in 1801. Encouraged by Sir Walter Scott she wrote *Letters from the Mountains* and *Essays on the Superstitions of the Highlands*.

1839 Kirkpatrick MacMillan of Courthill Smithy, Keirmill, Dumfriesshire, invented the pedal-driven bicycle. In 1842 he was fined 5 Scots shillings for speeding in Gorbals and knocking down a small girl on his 'devil on wheels'.

1840 Work commenced on the Scott Monument in Princes Street Gardens, Edinburgh. The architect, George Meikle Kemp, designed this Gothic steeple but sadly drowned in the Union Canal in 1844, two years before the building was completed. The statue in the base is of Sir Walter Scott with his favourite dog, Maida.

1841 The discovery of a new mineral, sulphate of cadmium, by Lord Greenock. The new mineral came to light during the excavation of the Bishopton tunnel, near Port Glasgow. Lord Greenock, who was also the 2nd Earl of Cathcart, owned the land.

1842 Allan Pinkerton, born in Glasgow, the son of a police sergeant, emigrated to America where he was to establish the world's most famous detective agency.

1843 Death of the famous Glasgow glutton, Rab Ha', who is buried in Gorbals cemetery. He once won a bet that he could eat an entire calf.

1844 The Glasgow Stock Exchange was inaugurated in rooms in Royal Exchange Square.

1845 'Colours' were given by Queen Victoria to the Duke of Atholl's Highland Regiment, the only private army in Britain.

1846 Potato famine in the Highlands resulting in the death of hundreds, and emigration to the Lowlands and the 'New World'.

1847 James Young Simpson, from Bathgate, discovered the anaesthetic properties of chloroform and advocated its general adoption. He faced public opposition based on the moral and physical implications of anaesthesia. This only changed when Queen Victoria's son, Leopold, was delivered under anaesthetic in 1853.

1848 The invention of the India rubber pneumatic tyre by William Robert Thomson, who was born in Stonehaven. Amongst many other inventions he patented the first steam traction engine in 1867.

1849 A lighthouse was built on Arnamurchan Point in Argyll (the most westerly part of mainland Britain).

1850 Birth of Robert Louis Stevenson, the author, in Edinburgh. Although his life was blighted by illness he travelled widely and produced many timeless books including *Treasure Island*, *Kidnapped* and *The Strange Case of Dr Jekyll and Mr Hyde*.

1851 The start of the world petroleum industry when Dr James 'Paraffin' Young opened the first ever refinery near Bathgate. He extracted paraffin from fossil-fuel-rich shales and coals.

1852   The last company in Britain running a sedan chair service closed in Edinburgh.

1853   Death of inventor James Chalmers of Arbroath. He proposed a standard postal charge and exhibited adhesive postage stamps in 1834, some six years prior to the introduction of the penny post by Rowland Hill.

1854   Birth of David Dunbar Buick in Arbroath. He emigrated to Detroit and founded a car manufacturing plant.

1855   Balmoral Castle, Deeside, was built for Queen Victoria. It was designed by William Smith of Aberdeen under the supervision of the Prince Consort.

1856   Birth of Sir Hugh Munro, the first Munro bagger! In 1891 he published his 'tables giving all the Scottish mountains exceeding 3000 ft in height' (914m). He died in Tarason, France, helping the wounded of the Great War.

1857 Publication of *The Coral Island* by Robert Michael Ballantyne, the children's writer. He was the nephew of James and John Ballantyne, printers and publishers to Sir Walter Scott.

1858 John Brown of Craithenaird, Balmoral, became Queen Victoria's personal servant and groom. Victoria was clearly devoted to him and was buried with a photograph of 'her beloved friend'.

1859 Birth of Sir Arthur Conan Doyle, in Edinburgh. Following a career as a ship's surgeon, he wrote various tales on his characters, Sherlock Holmes and Dr Watson.

1860 The birth of playwright and novelist JM Barrie at Kirriemuir, Angus. Amongst his many contributions to literature are *The Admirable Crichton* and his creation, Peter Pan.

1861 The first firing of the one o'clock gun in Edinburgh on 7th June 1861. Attempts on the previous two days had failed.

1862 Scotland was divided into 101 salmon fishery districts, each with the catchment area of a river or group of rivers.

1863 Death of Sir Colin Campbell, who was born Colin MacIver, the son of a Glasgow carpenter. He was an influential soldier and was in command of the Highland Brigade in the Crimea where he won the Battle of Alma. He inspired 'the thin red line' which held the Russian calvary at Balaclava.

1864 The three-masted barque, *City of Adelaide* was built. She started off life in the Australian wool trade but ultimately was renamed the *Carrick* SV and moored for many years beside the Broomielaw in Glasgow. It is now being restored at Irvine.

1865 The death of Scot 'James' Miranda Stuart Barry, who, because medicine was a career forbidden to women, masqueraded successfully as a man throughout her medical career . In 1857 she became the Inspector General of military hospitals in Montreal and Quebec.

1866 The 8th Marquis of Queensberry, the Scottish aristocrat Sir John Sholto Douglas, published a code of 12 rules to administer the noble art of boxing.

1867 Sir John MacDonald, a Glaswegian, became Canada's first Prime Minister.

1868 The first recorded hole-in-one was made by 'Young Tom' Morris, age 17 years and 5 months at the 8th hole at Prestwick, during the Open Championship. He won the Championship and also in the following three years. This feat has not been equalled.

1869 The sailing ship *Cutty Sark* was built by Scott and Linton at Dumbarton. Initially a tea clipper, she was then involved in the Australian woollen trade and is now moored permanently at Greenwich.

1870 Sir James Key Caird took over his father's jute and textile business in Dundee, at Ashton Mill. He prospered with the expansion in the linen and jute industries and made two large public donations leading to the creation of the hall and public park that bear his name in the city.

1871 The first rugby international under the 'Green Book' rules was played at Raeburn Place in Edinburgh. Scotland won the 20-a-side contest against England by a goal and a try to a try. This formed the basis for the Calcutta Cup matches between the countries which started eight years later.

1872 Death of Greyfriars' Bobby, the Skye terrier which, after the death of his master, 'Auld Jock', lay on or near his master's grave in Greyfriars' Churchyard for almost 14 years.

Stay!

Greyfriars Bobby

1873 Formation of the Scottish Football Association. The first members of the SFA were Queen's Park, Clydesdale, Vale of Leven, Dumbreck, Third Lanark Rifle Volunteer Reserves, Eastern, Granville and Rovers.

1874 Birth of Sir Hugh Roberton, the conductor of and arranger for the world-famous Glasgow Orpheus Choir.

1875 . First telephone call

1875 The first telephone call was made by the inventor Alexander Graham Bell, with the historic words, 'Come here, Mr Watson, I want to see you', spoken from an adjoining room to his assistant. Bell had emigrated to Boston from Edinburgh at the age of 23.

1876 Birth of Nigel Gresley in Edinburgh. He designed the world's fastest steam locomotives, the Flying Scotsman and the Mallard. The Mallard still holds the record for speed under steam: 126 mph in July 1938.

1877 The Blantyre pit explosion, Scotland's worst mining disaster, when 207 miners died.

1878 The crash of the City of Glasgow Bank. Three of its directors were imprisoned for fraud.

1879 The Tay Rail Bridge Disaster. Part of the single track bridge of almost two miles in length, collapsed under a train during a storm. The train was

recovered and put back into service but thereafter
nicknamed, The Diver.

Beautiful railway bridge of the silv'ry Tay!
Alas, I am very sorry to say
That ninety lives have been taken away
On the last sabbath day of 1879
Which will be remembered for a very long time.
William McGonagall, doggerel poet

1880 Birth of the composer, Francis George Scott, in
the Borders. He taught, amongst others, Hugh
MacDiarmid, setting many of the poet's words to
music.

1881 The 71st Highland Light Infantry and the 74th
Highlanders became the Highland Light Infantry.
The 91st Argyllshire Highlanders amalgamated with
the 93rd Sutherland Highlanders to become the
Argyll and Sutherland Highlanders; also the 42nd
Royal Highland Regiment amalgamated with the
73rd Perthshire to form the 'Black Watch'; and the
75th Stirling and the 92nd Gordons became the
'Gordon Highlanders'.

1882 The 'Battle of Braes', Isle of Skye, between crofters
and 50 Glasgow policemen. The 'battle' was over
crofting rights. Subsequent to this five men from
the Glendale crofting community were sentenced in
Edinburgh to two months imprisonment. They
became known as the 'Glendale Martyrs'.

1883 The founding of the Boys' Brigade in Glasgow, by
William Alexander Smith from Thurso.

1884 Birth of Peter Fraser in Fearn, Ross-shire. He emigrated to New Zealand in 1910 and became Prime Minister of New Zealand in 1940.

1885 Birth in Dundee of Will Fyffe, the character comedian, remembered best for his rendition of *I Belong to Glasgow*.

1886 Following unrest in crofting areas and the report of the Napier Commission, the Crofters' Holding Act was passed conferring on crofters security of tenure, a right to bequeath their tenancies and also, where appropriate, the right to rent arbitration.

1887 The late-Victorian whisky boom commenced. Over the next 13 years over 25 new distilleries opened in Speyside and the north of Scotland.

1888 The Scottish Parliamentary Labour Party was founded by James Keir Hardie. He was born in Holytown, a mining village near Motherwell. He started life in the pits, then opened a newsagents before writing for the radical press. By 1886 he was Secretary of the Scottish Miners' Federation. As an MP he was known as the 'Member for the Unemployed', wearing his famous cloth cap. (The Independent Labour Party was founded in Bradford in 1893.)

1889 The Mauricewood pit disaster at Penicuik, Midlothian, where 63 miners died when the wooden lining of a ventilation shaft caught fire.

1890 Opening of the Forth Railway Bridge spanning the Firth of Forth between South and North Queens-ferry. It took seven years to build with 57 men dying during its construction. (55,000 tons of steel, 62,000 cu ft of masonary, eight million rivets and 640,000 cu ft of Aberdeenshire granite were used.)

1891 An Comunn Gaidhealach, the Highland Association, was founded in Oban to further the study of Highland music, history and literature. The first National Mod was held in Oban the following year.

1892 Birth of Sir Robert Watson-Watt in Brechin whose interest in radio waves led to his historic recommendation, in 1935, that radar defences be set up; these ultimately played a major part in the winning of the Battle of Britain.

1893 Formation of Barr and Stroud Ltd. (Rangefinder and Instrument Developers and Manufacturers) by Professor Archibald Barr of Glenfield, near Paisley, and Professor of Physics, William Stroud.

1894 A Home Rule for Scotland Bill was passed in the House of Commons, but dropped when the Government fell.

1895 Birth of George MacLeod who won the MC and Croix de Guerre fighting as a captain in the Great War. He became a pacifist and went on to be a missionary, minister, founder of the Iona Community, Moderator of the General Assembly of the Church of Scotland, Chaplain to the Queen and a life peer.

1896 Start of the Glasgow Underground when a six and a half mile circuit was constructed. Originally powered by cable, the line was electrified to 600 volts in 1933. It was modernised over a period of three years between 1977-80. Its brightly coloured railway stock earned it the nickname 'Clockwork Orange'.

1897 Andrew Carnegie, the industrialist and philanthropist, purchased a Highland estate in Skibo in Sutherland. Born the son of a weaver in Dumfermline, his family emigrated to America in 1848. Through entrepreneurial acumen he made billions in the railroad and steel industries. The Carnegie Trust has donated millions of pounds throughout the world.

1898 Aberdeen's Cruikshank Botanic Gardens were established by Miss Anne Cruikshank, for the benefit of the University and the public.

1899 The Glasgow School of Art, designed by its architect, Charles Rennie Mackintosh, was completed.

20TH CENTURY

1900 The three keepers of the lighthouse on the Flannan Isles, Outer Hebrides, disappeared without trace.

1901 Soft drinks manufacturer, Andrew G Barr, developed the recipe for a new product made from fruit extract and iron salt, IRN BRU, which became known as 'Scotland's other national drink'.

1902 The Hill House in Helensburgh was designed by Charles Rennie Mackintosh for the publisher, WW Blackie. It is a modern translation of the traditional, functional Scottish house. It is now in the care of the National Trust for Scotland.

1903 Death of William Quarrier from Greenock, who began work at the age of seven in a pin factory. At 20 he started a boot and shoe manufacturing business. Quarrier devoted his life to looking after orphans, and founded Bridge of Weir Homes in 1876.

1904 The Nobel Prize for Chemistry was won by Sir William Ramsay of Glasgow ,whose research led to the discovery of neon and krypton and the foundation of nuclear science.

1905 The deathof Sir Richard Claverhouse Jebb from
Dundee, who was appointed Professor of Greek at
Glasgow and Cambridge Universities and
subsequently became the MP for Cambridge
University.

1906 The Cunard liner, *Lusitania*, built in only 14
months, was launched on the Clyde. She was
torpedoed and sunk in 1915 off the Old Head of
Kinsale, on the southern coast of Ireland.

1907 Two hundred and fifty five emigrants refused to
sail from Glasgow on the liner, *Astoria*. The reason
was she had only two funnels. The poster,
illustrating the ship, had shown three.

1908 Death of 'Old Tom' Morris, who was born in St
Andrews in 1821 and competed in every Open
Championship up to 1896. He won the Open four
times and remains the oldest winner, having won in
1867, aged 46.

1909 The Royal Commission on Whisky declared that
only spirits distilled in Scotland, from a mash
containing at least 30% malted barley, could legally
be called 'Scotch Whisky'.

1910   Glasgow School Board turned down a proposal, that pupils in State schools should be provided with free books and pencils.

1911   Strikes took place throughout Scotland , including a riot by dockers in Dundee. Twenty six boys were birched at Dunfermline Sheriff Court for malicious damage at the Jenny Gray Mine pithead.

1912   Death of Lord Joseph Lister, who as Professor of Surgery at the University of Glasgow, pioneered the benefits of disinfecting operating theatres and wards, primarily with carbolic acid.

1913   Birth of Benny Lynch in Glasgow, who became the Flyweight Boxing Champion of the World in 1935. He was the first Scot to win a world boxing title.

1914   Private Henry May of Bridgeton, in Glasgow, while serving with the First Scottish Rifles at La Boutullerie, won the Victoria Cross for bravery.

1915   Death of Mary Slessor, the missionary, in Calabar, Nigeria, age 67. Born in Aberdeen, her family moved to Dundee where she worked in the Jute Mills. In 1875 she applied to the Foreign Mission Board of the United Presbyterian Church for a posting to West Africa. At a remote station with no other missionaries nearby, she adopted children abandoned by their tribes. She was dearly loved and respected by the native population and, despite regular bouts of malaria, continued on with her work to the end.

1916   1916 Opening of the Princess Louise Hospital at Erskine, Renfrewshire. It is the largest ex-serviceman's hospital in Britain.

1917 The sinking of HMS *Vanguard*, moored at Scapa Flow in Orkney. It blew up as a result of unstable ammunition, killing 804 men . There were only two survivors.

1918 On Hogmanay the Admiralty vessel, *Iolaire* sailed from the Kyle of Lochalsh carrying 260 naval ratings home from the war. A gale blew up and the ship hit rocks at the entrance to Stornoway Harbour: 208 men, who had all survived the war, died within miles and sight of home.

1919 The 'Bloody Friday' riot took place in George Square, Glasgow, when strikers, wanting shorter working hours to offset the flooding of the labour market by demobilised soldiers, clashed with police. The following day tanks were on the streets of Glasgow and the strikers' leaders, Willie Gallacher and Emanuel Shinwell (who later became an MP), were imprisoned.

1920 Ex-Prime Minister, Herbert Asquith, who had lost his seat at the previous election, was returned as the MP for Paisley.

1921 The British Legion was created by Douglas Haig, 1st Earl Haig of Bemersyde. Born in Edinburgh he was appointed Commander-in-Chief of the British Forces in 1915. Although the actions ordered by him cost the lives of tens of thousands of servicemen, he devoted the rest of his life to the caring of the wounded and bereaved.

1922 Birth in Glasgow of Alistair MacLean, the novelist. Success in a *Glasgow Herald* short story competition and encouragement from an editor at

Collins, encouraged the Glasgow schoolteacher to
write his first novel in 1955, *HMS Ulysses*. His
many novels have sold over 200 million copies
worldwide. He died in Munich in 1987.

1923 Marriage of Elizabeth Bowes-Lyons, the daughter
of the Earl and Countess of Strathmore and
therefore a descendant of the ancient Kings of
Scotland, to the Duke of York (later George VI), at
Westminster Abbey.

1924 Eric Liddell won the Olympic Gold medal in the
400 metres in Paris. Known as the 'Flying Scotsman',
he had refused to run in the 100 metres because it had
been scheduled for a Sunday. He subsequently
became a missionary in China, and died of a brain
tumour in a Japanese internment camp in 1945.

1925 Murrayfield, the Scottish Rugby Union head-
quarters in Edinburgh, was inaugurated with a 14-
11 win over England.

1926 First transmission of televisual pictures as
demonstrated at the Royal Institution in London by
John Logie Baird, from Helensburgh, the inventor
of the medium. The first images transmitted were of
two ventriloquist's dummies, operated by Baird.

1927 Severe earthquake shook the east coast of Scotland;
from Dundee through to Orkney.

1928 Formation of the National Party of Scotland which
amalgamated in 1932 with the Scottish Party to
become the Scottish National Party. Its aim is to
restore Scottish Independence.

1929 Alexander Fleming of Loudoun, Ayrshire, published his historic paper in the *British Journal of Experimental Pathology*, announcing his discovery of penicillin. He was knighted in 1944.

1930 Death of Neil Munro, the novelist and journalist, who was born in Inveraray, Argyll. He wrote a number of historical novels but is best remembered for his tales of Para Handy and the motley crew of the Clyde puffer, the *Vital Spark*.

1931 The National Trust for Scotland was founded to promote the preservation of lands, buildings and places of national interest.

1932 Over 100 people reported sightings of the Loch Ness Monster. (A number of photographs were taken).

1933 The Marquis of Douglas and Clydesdale, who later became the Duke of Hamilton, piloted a Westland bi-plane on the first ever flight over Mount Everest.

1934 A mass exodus took place to Corby in Northamptonshire, by steel workers from Lanarkshire.

1935 Scotland's first full-time professional orchestra, the BBC Scottish Symphony Orchestra, was established in Edinburgh under the guidance of the BBC's Head of Music, Ian Whyte.

1936 The 81,000-ton liner Queen Mary, built at John Brown's shipyard in Clydebank, sailed down the Clyde on her maiden voyage. She was originally started in 1931 as No.'534' but work was halted due to the depression and not restarted until 1934. In 1939 she was converted into a troopship but returned to her Atlantic passenger route after the war and was withdrawn from service in 1967. She is now berthed at Long Beach, California as a museum and hotel.

1937 Death of Ramsay MacDonald of Lossiemouth who the first Labour Prime Minister of Great Britain, and served three terms of office between 1924 and 1935.

'We hear war called murder. It is not; it is suicide.' MacDonald in 1930.

1938 The Empire Exhibition was held in Bellahouston Park, Glasgow. 12,593,232 people attended it.

1939 The 'Churchill Barriers' were built in Orkney to block the east end of Scapa Flow between the mainland, Burray Island and South Ronaldsay. It was built following the torpedoing of *HMS Royal Oak* by a German submarine, No. U-47 with the loss of 810 lives.

1940 First daytime raid of the war by the German Luftwaffe on Glasgow. It resulted in little damage.

1941 The merchant ship, SS *Politician*, carrying 20,000 cases of whisky, foundered off the island of Eriskay in the Outer Hebrides. Islanders liberated an estimated 9,000 cases before the police and customs intervened. The venture was immortalised by Sir Compton MacKenzie in his novel, *Whisky Galore*.

1942 Due to the war effort, all driving of cars for pleasure was prohibited in Scotland.

1943 The Citizens' Theatre Company was founded by a board including Dr Henry Mavor. Its first production was *The Holy Isle* by James Bridie (the pseudonym of Dr Mavor). The theatre is located in Gorbals, Glasgow.

1944 First 'prefabs' erected for bombed-out families in Scotland. They were steel built, single-storey buildings with two bedrooms, living room, kitchen and bathroom.

1945 Doctor Robert McIntyre from Lanarkshire, became the first Scottish Nationalist MP by winning the Motherwell by-election. He died in February, 1998.

1946 The PS *Waverley*, now the last sea-going paddle steamer in the world, was built by A&J Inglis for service on the Clyde.

1947 The launch of the International Festival of Music and Drama in Edinburgh. Amongst the 800 performers were the Vienna Philharmonic Orchestra and the singer, Kathleen Ferrier.

1948 The weekly milk ration was increased by a pint to three and a half pints. (It was reduced again the following year to two pints.)

1949 John Boyd-Orr from Kilmaurs, in Ayrshire, who became the Director-General for the United Nations Food and Agricultural Organisation, won the Nobel Peace Prize.

1950 Death of Sir Harry Lauder, who was born in Portobello, and initially worked in a coal mine in Hamilton. He won first prize in a singing contest and went on to be a world-famous entertainer. He is remembered particularly for his songs, *I Love A Lassie, Roamin' in the Gloamin'* and *Keep Right on to the End of the Road.*

1951 Stone of Scone deposited in Arbroath Abbey. It had been removed from Westminster Abbey, by a group of Scottish students, on Christmas Eve 1950. (See 1296)

1952 BBC television service started in Scotland with the opening of the Kirk o' Shotts transmitter. (41,000 TV sets were in existence in Scotland at this time).

1953 Loss of the car ferry, *Princess Victoria*, in a severe storm on the Stranraer to Larne route. 133 people were drowned; 41 were saved.

1954 Britain's first fast breeder nuclear reactor, was built on the site of a World War Two airfield, at Dounreay, Caithness.

1955 Scotland's first independent television company, STV, started transmitting.

1956 Dick Taggart, of Dundee, won the gold medal at lightweight for boxing, at the Melbourne Olympic Games.

1957 Death of Sir William Craigie from Dundee, the editor of the *New English Dictionary*.

1958 The trial of the mass murderer, Peter Manuel, at the High Court of Justiciary in Glasgow. Charged with eight murders, he dismissed his Counsel after nine days of the 14-day trial. Although the judge said that 'the accused had presented his case with a skill that was remarkable', he was found guilty and hanged at Barlinnie Prison, Glasgow.

1959 Auchengeich pit disaster at Chryston, Lanarkshire, when an underground fire caused the death of 47 miners.

1960 The American nuclear submarine base was established in the Holy Loch, near Dunoon on the Clyde. It remained there until 1992.

1961 A steel strip mill was established at Ravenscraig; also the Linwood car plant, which produced the famous Hillman Imp.

1962 The last tramcar ran in Glasgow, from Dalmuir to Auchenshuggle.

1963 Dr Richard Beeching announced that 435 of Scotland's 660 passenger stations were to be closed.

1964 The opening of the Forth Road Bridge by the Queen Mother. The first toll was half-a-crown (two shillings and sixpence, or 12.5p.)

1965 Establishment of the Highlands and Islands Development Board.

1966 Chay Blyth of Hawick, and John Ridgeway, rowed across the Atlantic.

1967 The first oil well was drilled in the Scottish sector of the North Sea. (The first major find was the Forties field, 100 miles off Aberdeen, in 1970.)

1968 A hurricane, with winds gusting up to 140 mph, devastated Scotland. Many roofs, chimneys and houses collapsed; 21 people were killed and hundreds injured.

1969 Birth in Edinburgh of Stephen Hendry, the world snooker champion. He won the Scottish Amateur Championship at the age of 15 and in 1987 became the youngest ever winner of a professional title. In 1990, as the youngest world champion, he started his run of championship wins.

1970 The opening of the Kingston Bridge over the Clyde, between Anderston and Kingston. It carries the M8 and is deemed to the busiest motorway bridge in Europe.

1971 The Ibrox disaster, when 66 football fans died on stairway 13, at Ibrox Stadium, Glasgow towards the end of an 'Old Firm' match.

1972 End of the Upper Clyde Shipbuilders 'work-in' which had started the previous year at the Clydebank, Govan, Linthouse and Scotstoun yards. It had been brought about by the Government committing to reduce public subsidies to ailing shipyards. Led by their leaders, Jimmy Reid and Jimmy Airlie, the workforce overcame demarcation rulings between the unions and installed standards and discipline to ensure shipbuilding continued. The 'work-in' ended in a takeover bid by the Texas-based group, Marathon.

1973 Jackie Stewart, from Dunbartonshire, won his third world championship in Grand Prix motor racing and retired; he had previously won in 1969 and 1971.

1974 A record eleven Scottish Nationalist Members of Parliament were returned to Westminster, having obtained 30.4% of the votes cast in Scotland.

1975 A local government reorganisation in Scotland was implemented as a result of the Wheatley Report. Lord Wheatley had recommended a 'tier' system of local government consisting of seven regions and 37 districts, thereby abolishing the county councils which had been in existence since 1889.

1976 As a result of the Clayton Report, drinking hours were changed in Scotland allowing most licensed outlets to remain open between 11.00am and 11.00pm.

1977 Scotland beat England 2-1 at Wembley Stadium; fans dug up parts of the pitch as souvenirs.

1978 Oil was piped to Sullum Voe in Shetland, Britain's largest oil terminal. Two massive submarine pipelines brought in crude oil from the East Shetland Basin before it was shipped out to refineries.

1979 A referendum on devolution was held in Scotland. 51.6% of Scots voted yes on a 63% turnout. Since 40% of elegible voters were required for it to succeed, home rule failed to get off the ground.

1980 Twenty-eight-year-old Allan Wells, from Edinburgh, won gold medal at the Moscow Olympics when he won the 100m in 10.25 seconds.

1981 The death of Scotland's most quotable footballing hero, Bill Shankly. As the manager of Liverpool FC, he laid the foundations for the club's subsequent success in Europe.

'Me havin' no education, I had to use my brains.'

1982 The first meeting on Scottish soil between the Moderator of the General Assembly of the Church of Scotland and the Pope. It took place at the Kirk's Assembly Hall in Edinburgh.

1983 The Burrell Collection in the Pollok Estate, Glasgow was opened by Queen Elizabeth II. The catholic collection was amassed by the ship owner and art collector, Sir William Burrell (1861-1958).

1984 Mine strikes and closures took place in Scotland and throughout the UK. The leading protagonists were two Scots: Ian MacGregor, the Chairman of the National Coal Board and Mick McGahey, the President of the Scottish Mineworkers.

1985 Death of the 'Tall Droll', the innovative comic genius, Chic Murray, from Greenock.

'I was standing at the bus stop the other day when a

man came up to me and said, "Have you got a light, mac?" I said, "No, but I've got a dark brown overcoat".'

1986 Return of the *Discovery* to Dundee. The ship had been built in Dundee for the National Antarctic Expedition and was launched in 1901. Commanded by Capt Robert F Scott, it sailed to Antarctica and spent several years in the ice. After a number of years engaged in scientific research and after service with the Sea Scouts and also as part of a Maritime Museum in London, she was brought back to Dundee.

1987 Nurse Susan Wighton, of Glasgow, was named 'Scot of the Year', and lauded for her caring work among Palestinian refugees in the beseiged Beiruit camp of Bourj-al-Barajneh.

1988 Two major disasters in Scotland. The Piper Alpha oil rig, owned by Occidental Oil, went on fire with the loss of 167 men. Then the Lockerbie air disaster when a Pan Am Boeing 747 exploded and crashed on the town of Lockerbie in Dumfriesshire. 243 passengers,16 crew and 11 Lockerbie residents were killed. (Just 20 miles south of Locherbie, in 1915, Britain's worst rail disaster occurred; three trains collided with the loss of 227 lives.)

1989 Knighthood for the daring Scots pioneer of the SAS, Col David Stirling. When successive British Commanders were being defeated by the Germans in North Africa in 1941, he formed a raiding group. Using American jeeps armed with twin machine-guns, the fledgling SAS attacked German airfields behind the enemy lines, planting bombs on parked planes and fuel dumps. He was captured in 1943 and finished his war in Colditz.

1990 The Scottish rugby team overcome all odds to defeat the English by 13 points to 7 at Murrayfield and thus secure the Grand Slam, the Calcutta Cup and the Triple Crown for the first time in the game's history.

1991 Historic Scotland founded as as the executive agency looking after over 300 historic properties, including Edinburgh Castle. It also lists buildings and monuments worthy of conservation, excavating historic sites and granting aid for the repair and preservation of ancient buildings.

1992 Holy Island, Lamlash Bay, Arran, purchased by the Samye Ling Buddhist Monastery of Eskdalemuir, as a retreat.

1993 The *Braer*, an 89,000-ton Liberian-registered tanker, ran aground in a 100mph gale in Quendale Bay, west of Sumburgh Head in Shetland. All its oil spilled into the sea.

1994 John Smith, the 14th Leader of the Labour Party, died of a heart attack in London. He was buried on Iona.

1995 Scotland's golfers won the Alfred Dunhill Cup at St Andrews.

1996 The Stone of Destiny returned to Scotland from Westminster Abbey (see 1296 and 1951). It arrived at Edinburgh Castle on St Andrews Day and is now on display.

1997   Scotland voted, on the 700th anniversary of William Wallace's victory at Stirling Bridge, to have its own Parliament again. 74.2% of Scots supported a devolved Parliament with 63.4% giving support for limited tax raising powers: the turnout amongst Scotland's eligible voters was 60.1%.

1998   The opening of the imposing new museum of Scotland, situated at the corner of Edinburgh's Chambers Street and George IV Bridge. Deemed to be the most important building constructed in Scotland for decades, it houses the merged collections of the National Museum of Antiquities in Scotland and the Royal Scottish Museum.

1999   Glasgow designated UK City of Architecture and Design. Major projects include the conversion of the former *Herald* building – Charles Rennie Mackintosh's first major design -- to form a permanent home for the 'Lighthouse', Scotland's centre for architecture, design and the city. This provides an influential worldwide model for the interpretation of architecture and design.

THE NEW MILLENNIUM

2000 The start of the new millennium … Scotland's
Parliament has recommenced after 293 years.
A nation again!

O Scotia, my dear; my native soil,
For whom my warmest wish to heaven is sent!
Long may thy hardy sons of rustic toil
Be blest with health, and peace, and sweet content!
And oh, may heaven their simple lives prevent
From luxury's contagion, weak and vile!
Then, howe'er crowns and coronets be sent
A virtuous populace may rise the while,
And stand a wall of fire around this much-loved isle.

Robert Burns
The Cotter's Saturday Night

25th Jan 3001